EX LIBRIS

Investing in Scottish Pictures

A handy pocket-size guide to collecting and
purchasing Scottish paintings
incorporating

Brief biographies of some 480 Scottish painters
born before 1900

Price guide to Scottish paintings sold in 1976

Appraisal of market trends and developments

Uniform with this volume

The Glasgow School of Painting: David Martin
Three Scottish Colourists: T. J. Honeyman

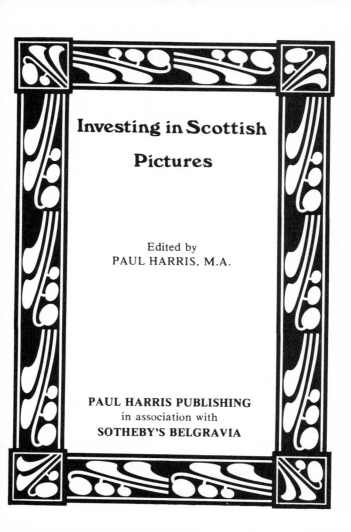

Investing in Scottish

Pictures

Edited by
PAUL HARRIS, M.A.

PAUL HARRIS PUBLISHING
in association with
SOTHEBY'S BELGRAVIA

Published jointly 1977 by
Paul Harris Publishing
25 London Street
Edinburgh
and
Sotheby's Belgravia
London and Edinburgh

ISBN 0 904505 18 9

Printed in Scotland by
Lindsay & Co. Ltd., Edinburgh

HOW TO USE THIS BOOK

This pocket reference guide lists some 480 Scottish painters born before 1900. As with our *Concise Dictionary of Scottish Painters*, published last year, we have decided to limit our selection in this way so as to avoid invidious value judgments as to whom to include from the wide-ranging field of contemporary artists. This is rendered even more necessary this time as, most often, auction prices for contemporary Scottish artists are volatile and misleading.

The figures printed at the end of the brief biographies in this book are drawn from prices achieved in Scottish auction rooms during 1976; that is to say, the sales of Phillips (Edinburgh), Lyon and Turnbull (Edinburgh), Edmiston's (Glasgow), Morrison McChlery (Glasgow) and the Sotheby's Belgravia sales held in Scotland at Scone Palace, Gleneagles Hotel and the Central Hotel, Glasgow. These are the auction houses which hold regular sales of predominantly Scottish pictures. Occasionally a 1975 price is indicated and this is distinguished by (1975).

Those who regularly attend auction sales will appreciate only too well a certain disparity at times between attribution and description in the catalogue, on the one hand, and their own opinion upon examining the actual lot. For the purpose of making this guide as useful and accurate as possible either I, personally, or a personal representative, have attended every sale at these auction houses and where, in our opinion, a picture was wrongly attributed or of doubtful origin its price has not been included.

Where a number of pictures by a given artist were sold during the year a price range is given — the lowest figure being the lowest price achieved and the highest representing the top price. A single figure will normally indicate that only one picture was sold subject, of course, to our qualification of examination and satisfaction as to correct cataloguing. No prices under £10 have been registered as we did not feel it would be useful to so do. All prices are expressed in pounds sterling and relate to oil paintings unless indicated otherwise with a letter in brackets as follows: (W) Watercolour, (P) Pastel, (D) Drawing.

Finally, a cautionary note. Prices achieved by pictures vary enormously depending on a number of important factors such as condition, physical size and the dexterity with which a particular picture has been executed. Many well-known and sought-after artists had "poor" periods or produced untypical, substandard pictures; quite rightly such efforts will receive poor prices at auction, giving a wide range to the prices indicated here. Although this book can give an accurate reflection of recent prices for most Scottish painters it should not be used as an absolute guide as to what to pay for some future purchase. Every picture is an individual creation and it is, so as to speak, worth what it is worth to the purchaser. If a picture is to one's particular taste and liking I would suggest it should be bought at a price within the band indicated in this book; the top end of the band should only be exceeded if one is completely sure of its suitability. Otherwise, there is considerable danger of making a bad investment. However, that is not to say I would recommend the purchase of pictures purely for investment. The primary objective should be to single out those pictures which make some personal appeal and which will serve to give enjoyment and enrichment; thus selected, a picture should be bought within the boundary of sensible price and one should then have a most sound investment, as well as an object of beauty.

MARKET TRENDS AND DEVELOPMENTS

It is said that the art and antiques market is the first to feel the effects of a serious recession such as that which we are suffering currently. If that is the case, I would venture to suggest that we are now climbing out of the slough of despond for 1976 was not the sort of year one might have expected in the auction room with the economic disasters which followed one another with monotonous regularity. Despite unemployment, business collapses and the sinking pound, prices for Scottish pictures remained reasonably steady and, in many instances, rose quite remarkably.

Although the days are now over when an **E. A. Hornel** happily fetched £5,000-£6,000 (and they will no doubt come again) the vast majority of pictures in the top price range held steady and there was, indeed, evidence of some artists such as **J. Lawton Wingate, Tom Campbell, Walter Hugh Paton** and **William Miller Frazer** really taking off and moving into distinctly higher price brackets; purchase of any of these artists a couple of years ago would now represent a most sound investment. Artists already in a higher bracket held up remarkably well; **William MacTaggart, Gemmell Hutchison** and the **Nasmyths** all maintained their level and remain as popular and sought after as ever. **Hornel** failed to show up well during the year with prices around the £2,000 mark until Edmiston's December sale where MacNicol of Glasgow paid £3,400 for a particularly attractive example of the artist's work. At present prices Hornels must now be a good buy.

Indeed, most members of the Glasgow School must be under-valued. With the exception of **David Gauld**, whose ubiquitous sulking cattle appear with monotonous regularity, and **Stuart Park's** luminous flowerpieces, good Glasgow School pictures do not appear often and, to my mind, are not done justice by the prices achieved. Paintings by **James Elder Christie, George Henry, Sir James Guthrie, Thomas Corsan Morton, J. Whitelaw Hamilton** and other members of the School should be pursued relentlessly.

A few names appeared to flood the market at times. Dozens of dismal watercolours and a few quite good oils by **Thomas Bunting** appeared as from nowhere and watercolours by **Henry Wright Kerr** started the year well but were unable to find bidders by the latter half of the year.

It is to be noted with regret that **Stanley Cursiter** and **Adam Bruce Thomson** passed away during the year. Such is the nature of the art market this will inevitably affect performance of their pictures at auction. Indeed, an extremely good price was paid at Phillips in October for a Cursiter oil of waves breaking upon rocks.

Many artists have firmly established price levels based upon pictures of a consistently high quality having appeared regularly. One might mention **David Farquharson, Joseph Farquharson, James Kay** and **Robert McGregor**. If I had to make some tips for names to join them in the future I might suggest **Joe Milne, William Mervyn Glass, Nicol Laidlaw, William Wells** and those Glasgow artists connected with the arts and crafts movement in Glasgow after the turn of the century. This last field of interest is due to be popularised by a rash of published material over the next couple of years.

One of the outstanding sales of 1977 must be the sale of the contents of **Jessie M. King's** studio by Sotheby's in Scotland and this will serve to draw further attention to the remarkable flowering of artistic endeavour in the West of Scotland after 1900. Indeed, **Jessie M. King** is already firmly established on the international map (as **Charles Rennie Mackintosh** was long before being recognised in his own country). So the work of **Katherine Cameron, Annie French, Fra. Newbery, Louise Perman** and others of that group should be watched with care.

By way of a final and more general comment I should like to state my sure and certain conviction that quality Scottish pictures are still undervalued in the context of the international art market. Paintings by artists of the Glasgow School and the Colourists (**Peploe, Cadell, Hunter** and **Fergusson**) are important in a European setting; the former group was not only influenced by the great European Schools of the late nineteenth century and produced a series of Scottish Impressionist pictures on a par with their European counterparts (and still largely undervalued), but was, itself, of seminal importance in later developments in Munich and Vienna, for example. In terms of quality many Scottish pictures of this period are quite as good, if not better, than those executed by more famous Continental counterparts. This is already being realised by European buyers attracted by paintings of Continental subjects painted by the Glasgow School and the Colourists; it can only be a matter of time before they move on to subjects of less obvious direct appeal. Indeed, many fine Scottish pictures have recently been exported to Japanese buyers to whom the quality is evident, despite the difference in cultures.

It is to be fervently hoped that the works of Scotland's outstanding artists do not flood out of the country in the next few years and that, instead, indigenous purchasers will appear. *For there can be little doubt that not only are quality Scottish paintings of the last hundred years undervalued in the context of the international art market, but they still represent an outstanding investment which will provide a considerably greater return than, for example, the stock market or other such traditional forms of investment.* Crystal-ball gazing is always dangerous, but through the mists of economic depression I see Scottish pictures regarded as expensive today increasing in value astronomically as the severe limits to the available pool are realised, and as more examples of the finest work go to ready buyers in Europe, the United States and Japan.

Paul Harris
25 London Street
Edinburgh
January 1977

Advice on the sale, purchase or valuation of paintings
is given by

John Robertson
Sotheby's representative
19 Castle Street
Edinburgh, EH2 3AH
031-226 5438

or by Sotheby's Belgravia, 19 Motcomb Street
London, SW1X 8LB
Telephone: 01-235 4311 (contact Peter Nahum)

ABBREVIATIONS
(Foundation dates in brackets)

A.R.S.A.	Associate of The Royal Scottish Academy
R.S.A.	(Royal 1838) Scottish Academician (1826)
P.R.S.A.	President of The Royal Scottish Academy
H.R.S.A.	Honorary Member of The Royal Scottish Academy
R.S.W.	Royal Scottish Society of Painters in Watercolours (1878)
P.R.S.W.	President of The Royal Scottish Society of Painters in Watercolours.
S.S.A.	Society of Scottish Artists (1891)
A.R.A.	Associate of the Royal Academy
R.A.	Royal Academician (1786)
H.R.A.	Honorary Royal Academician
R.B.A.	(Royal 1887) Society of British Artists (1824)
R.E.	(Royal 1888) Society of Painter-Etchers (1880)
A.R.H.A.	Associate of The Royal Hibernian Academy
R.H.A.	Royal Hibernian Academician (1823)
R.I.	(Royal 1884) Institute of Painters in Watercolours (1832)
R.W.S.	Member of The (Royal 1881) Society of Painters in Watercolours
R.P.	Member of The Royal Society of Portrait Painters (1804)
G.S.A.	Glasgow School of Art (1891)
R.C.A.	Royal College of Art
e.	elder (son)
fl.	active (flourished)

ADAM, JOSEPH DENOVAN (1842-1896). Born, Glasgow; exhibited R.S.A., 1871-1896; Highland landscapes, cattle and farming scenes. A.R.S.A., 1884; R.S.A., 1892. Died, Glasgow. **£35-160.**

ADAM, PATRICK WILLIAM (1845-1929). Born, Edinburgh; studied at R.S.A. Schools, later in London; painted landscapes, portraiture, but mainly interiors. A.R.S.A., 1883; R.S.A., 1897. Died, North Berwick. **£100-180.**

AFFLECK, ANDREW F. (fl. 1910-1935). Exhibited R.S.A. and Glasgow Institute; painter and etcher; best subjects: architectural.

AGNEW, ERIC MUNRO (born 1887). Born, Kirkcaldy; studied G.S.A. and Slade; painter and designer.

AIKEN, JOHN MACDONALD (1880-1961). Born, Aberdeen; studied Grays School of Art and Head there 1911-1914; principally known for his portraits but also designed stained glass. A.R.S.A., 1923; R.S.A., 1936.

AIKMAN, GEORGE (1830-1905). Exhibited R.A. and London galleries; worked as engraver and painted portraits and landscapes; A.R.S.A., 1880. Died, Edinburgh. **£20-200.**

AIKMAN, WILLIAM (1682-1731). Born, Cairney, Forfarshire; studied portraiture in Edinburgh under Sir John Medina; after travel to Rome, Constantinople and Syria, succeeded to Medina's practice, but worked in London from 1723; friend of Walpole, Swift, Gay, Pope and Thomson. Died, London.

ALEXANDER, COSMO JOHN (1724-1773?). Son of John Alexander; portrait painter; "out" in the '45; probably in Italy after the Rebellion.

ALEXANDER, EDWIN J. (1870-1926). Born, Edinburgh; e. son of R. Alexander, R.S.A. (*q.v.*); studied Edinburgh and Paris; painted birds and animal subjects. A.R.S.A., 1902; R.S.A., 1913; R.W.S. Died Musselburgh. **£14, 15-300 (w).**

ALEXANDER, JOHN (dates uncertain). Grandson or great-grandson of George Jamesone (*q.v.*). Made a series of etchings after Raphael, 1712; decorated part of Gordon Castle; painted chiefly portraits. *c.* 1690-1760.

ALEXANDER, ROBERT (1840-1923). Born, Dalgaren, Ayrshire; apprentice to a house-painter, then in workshop of Royal Scottish Museum; ultimately painted domestic animals. A.R.S.A., 1878; R.S.A., 1888; R.S.W., 1889-1901. Died, Slateford, Edinburgh. **£360 (1975).**

ALISON, DAVID (1882-1954). Lived in Fife and Edinburgh; painted portraits almost exclusively. A.R.S.A., 1916.

ALISON, HENRY Y. (*fl.* 1920-1950). Exhibited R.S.A. and Glasgow Institute; portraits and landscapes in oil; lived, Glasgow and Ayrshire. **£21-45.**

ALLAN, DAVID (1744-1796). Born, Alloa; Foulis's Glasgow Academy of Art; gold medal of Academy of St Luke in Rome; London, 1777; Edinburgh, 1780; first painted peasant life and character, then Scottish manners and customs; friend and illustrator of Burns.   Died, Edinburgh.

ALLAN, ROBERT W. (1852-1942).   Born, Glasgow; early 1880s went to live in London and became a leading member of the R.W.S.; travelled extensively in Europe and India (1891-1892); exhibited R.S.A.; watercolours and oils of harbours, landscape and seascapes. **£52-720, 72-110 (w).**

ALLAN, SIR WILLIAM (1782-1850).   Born, Edinburgh; studied with Wilkie under Graham, then at R.A. School, London; painted portraits in St Petersburg, painted historical scenes, and succeeded Wilkie in 1842 as Her Majesty's Limner for Scotland.   A.R.A., 1826; R.A., 1835; R.S.A., 1829; P.R.S.A., 1838.   Died, Edinburgh. **£100-350.**

ANDERSON, ROBERT (1842-1885).   Lived in Edinburgh and travelled in France, Holland and Spain; initially a line engraver who turned to painting in watercolour in the last years of his life; harbours and fishing scenes predominate. A.R.S.A., 1879.

ARCHER, JAMES (1823-1904).   Born, Edinburgh; studied at Trustees' Academy; moved to London, 1864; painted historical and romantic pictures, but chiefly portraits, often in crayon.   A.R.S.A., 1850; R.S.A., 1858.   Died, Haslemere. **£100 (1975).**

ARMOUR,   GEORGE   DENHOLM   (1864-1949). Sporting and hunting pictures, also book illustration. **£140, 80 (w).**

BALLANTYNE, JOHN (1815-1897). First exhibited R.S.A. at age of 16 and then consistently until 1887; lived and worked in Edinburgh 1831-1862; thereafter London. A.R.S.A., 1841; R.S.A., 1860.

BALLINGALL, ALEXANDER (*fl.* 1880-1910). Painter of seascapes and harbour scenes in watercolour; painted widely in Scotland **£40-100 (w).**

BALMAIN, KENNETH FIELD (born 1890). Born, Edinburgh; studied Edinburgh College of Art and R.S.A.; exhibited R.S.A., S.S.A.

BANNATYNE, JOHN JAMES (1836-1911). Exhibited R.S.A., 1859-1902; also R.A., R.I. and Suffolk St.; landscape painter of Scottish views; R.S.W. **£38 (1975).**

BARCLAY, JOHN MACLAREN (1811-1886). Lived and worked in Edinburgh and Perth; specialised in portraiture. A.R.S.A., 1863; R.S.A., 1871. **£120.**

BARNARD, MARY B. (1870-1946). Born, Wiltshire; married Duncan MacGregor Whyte 1901; lived Glasgow and Oban; exhibited Paris Salon, England and Scotland. Died, Oban.

BEATON, PENELOPE (1886-1963). Born, Edinburgh; studied Edinburgh College of Art; taught at Hamilton Academy before joining staff of Edinburgh College of Art in 1919. A.R.S.A., 1957; R.S.W., 1952. Died, Edinburgh.

SAMUEL JOHN PEPLOE (1871-1935)
Still Life
Sold by Sotheby's in Scotland
£5,600

ALEXANDER GOUDIE (born 1933)
Still Life
Sold by Sotheby's in Scotland
£1,300

BELL, JOHN ZEPHENIAH (1794-1883). Studied in Paris and worked in Edinburgh, Rome, Lisbon, Oporto and Manchester; Scottish domestic and historical scenes. R.S.A., 1829.

BELL, ROBERT P. (1841-1931). Lived and worked in Edinburgh and Hamilton; specialised in portraiture and genre painting. A.R.S.A., 1880.

BLACK, ANDREW (1850-1916). Born and worked in Glasgow. R.S.W. **£20-50, 450 (1975).**

BLACKLOCK, THOMAS BROMLEY (1863-1903). Born, Kirkcudbright; studied in Edinburgh; painted chiefly at East Linton; first, pure landscape, then with figures introduced, and lastly fairytales. **£75-280.**

BLAIR, JOHN (*fl.* 1870-1910). Exhibited R.S.A., 1870-1912; lived in Edinburgh; painted Scottish landscapes; book illustration. **£30-40 (w).**

BLATHERWICK, LILY (1872-1935). Painter of Scottish landscapes; founder member of the R.S.W.; married the artist A. S. Hartrick in 1896; painted flowers and small creatures in addition to landscape work. Died, London. **£22 (w).**

BOGLE, JOHN (*c.* 1746-1805). Born, Scotland; early work done in Glasgow and Edinburgh; miniature painter; moved to London, where he died in poverty.

BONE, SIR MUIRHEAD (1876-1953). Born, Glasgow; studied G.S.A.; established R.A. from 1908; official war artist in both World Wars; admired for prints and etchings, also book illustration. Hon. A.R.I.B.A.; Hon. R.S.A.; Hon. R.W.S.; Hon. R.E. Died, Oxford. **£20-42 (d), 50 (w).**

BONNAR, WILLIAM (1800-1853).   Born, Edinburgh; painted romantic and pastoral subjects, portraits and historical scenes; influence of Wilkie apparent in genre paintings. R.S.A., 1829. Died, Edinburgh.

BORTHWICK, ALFRED EDWARD (1871-1955).   Born, Scarborough; studied Edinburgh, London and Paris; travelled extensively abroad; portraits and allegorical works. R.S.A.; P.R.S.W.

BOUGH, SAMUEL (1822-1878).   Born, Carlisle; in 1845, scene-painter at Theatre Royal, Manchester, later in Glasgow, where he went in 1848 as a landscape painter, and in Edinburgh, where he settled in 1855; practically self-taught; painted in oil and watercolour. A.R.S.A., 1856; R.S.A., 1875. Died, Edinburgh. **£18-2,100, 45-60 (w).**

BOWIE, JOHN DICK (1860-1941). Lived and worked in Edinburgh up until 1913 when he moved to London; exhibited R.S.A.. 1882-1916; A.R.S.A., 1903.

BRIGGS, ERNEST EDWARD (1866-1913).   Born, Broughty Ferry; studied Slade School, 1883-87; exhibited R.A. from 1889; author of *Angling and Art in Scotland* (1912) and friend of J. Sydney Steel (*q.v.*); R.I.; R.S.W. Died, Dunkeld.

BRODIE, WILLIAM (1815-1881). Born, Banff; settled in Edinburgh, 1847, studied in Rome, 1853; sculptor. A.R.S.A., 1851; R.S.A., 1859. Died, Edinburgh.

BROUGH, ROBERT (1872-1905). Born, Invergordon; Aberdeen Art School; R.S.A. Life Class; under Constant in Paris; from 1894, portrait painter in Aberdeen and London. A.R.S.A., 1904. Died as a result of a railway accident near Sheffield.

BROWN, ALEXANDER KELLOCK (1849-1922). Born, Edinburgh; textile designer; Haldane Academy, Glasgow, where he chiefly lived and worked as a landscape painter. A.R.S.A., 1892; R.S.A., 1908; R.S.W., 1878. Died at Lamlash, Arran. **£40, 26 (w)**.

BROWN, JOHN (1752-1787). Born, Edinburgh; in 1771 went to Italy as draughtsman for Townley and William Young; a portraitist in Edinburgh and London; well known for his heads in pencil. Died, Leith.

BROWN, JOHN CRAWFORD (1805-1867). Worked in Glasgow, 1830-1841, thereafter in Edinburgh; exhibited R.S.A., 1830-1880; landscapes and genre paintings. A.R.S.A., 1843.

BROWN, J. MICHAEL. Edinburgh painter; exhibited R.S.A., 1879-1906. **£50 (1975)**.

BROWN, THOMAS AUSTEN (1857-1924). Born, Edinburgh; R.S.A. Schools; pioneer in Glasgow School movement. Painted pastoral and similar subjects. Died, Boulogne. **£60**.

BROWN, WILLIAM BEATTIE (1831-1909). Born Haddington; lived and worked in Edinburgh; exhibited R.S.A., 1852-1910; prolific painter of Scottish scenes in sombre colours. A.R.S.A., 1871; R.S.A., 1884. Died, Edinburgh. **£55-130.**

BROWN, WILLIAM MARSHALL (1863-1936). Born, Edinburgh; as youth, worked at wood engraving and book illustration; studied in R.S.A. Life School, 1884-88; painted landscapes and figure-subjects in Holland, Belgium, France and Scotland; studies of children at leisure probably represented his work at its best. A.R.S.A., 1909; R.S.A., 1928; R.S.W., 1929. **£22-500.**

BUCHANAN, PETER S. (*fl.* 1870-1890). Exhibited R.S.A., 1868-1891.

BUNTING, THOMAS (1851-1928). Born, Aberdeen; painted views in watercolour and oil in and around Aberdeen; rather muted, muddied colours. **£48-90, 26 (w).**

BURNET, JAMES M. (1788-1816). Born, Musselburgh; Scottish scenes.

BURNET, JOHN (1784-1868). Born, Musselburgh; painter and engraver; "Pensioners celebrating the Battle of Waterloo" painted for Duke of Wellington in 1837; wrote on art and art subjects. Died, Stoke Newington.

BURNS-MURDOCH, W. L. (1862-1939). Studied Antwerp, Paris, Florence, Naples and Madrid; exhibited

R.A. from 1891 and R.S.A.; Paris Salon; painted and travelled widely; lived and died in Edinburgh. **£50.**

BURNS, ROBERT (1869-1941). Born, Edinburgh; influenced by the Celtic revival and contributed to *The Evergreen;* later visited North Africa; illustrated and published books 1937 and 1940. A.R.S.A., 1902 (resigned 1920). Died, Edinburgh. **£145, 42 (w).**

BURR, ALEXANDER HOHENLOHE (1835-1899). Born, Edinburgh; brother of john Burr (*q.v.*); Trustees' Academy; settled in London, 1861; exhibited scenes of domestic life at R.S.A. and R.A.

BURR, GORDON G. (*fl.* 1890s). Painted watercolours in Aberdeen and area during the 1890s.

BURR, JOHN (1831-1893). Born, Edinburgh; elder brother of A. H. Burr (*q.v.*); Trustees' Academy; settled in London, 1861; exhibited scenes of domestic life at R.S.A. and R.A.; A.R.W.S., 1883; P.R.B.A. Died, London. **£200-220, 1,000 (1975).**

BURTON, MUNGO (1799-1882). Lived and worked in Edinburgh; painted portraits almost exclusively. A.R.S.A., 1845.

CADELL, FLORENCE ST. JOHN (*c.* 1880-1968). Born, Edinburgh; studied in Paris at the turn of the century where she executed some fine work in oil; landscapes, portraits and animals (espec. goats). Died, Edinburgh.

CADELL, FRANCES CAMPBELL BOILEAU (1883-1937). Born, Edinburgh; served in Great War, 1916-19; painted landscapes, portraits and still-life. A.R.S.A., 1931; R.S.A., 1936; R.S.W., 1935. Member of Royal Society of Portrait Painters. Died, Edinburgh. **£380-2,000, 45-170 (w).**

CADENHEAD, JAMES (1858-1927). Born, Aberdeen; studied at Trustees' Academy, R.S.A. Life School and Paris; painted landscapes in oil and watercolour; A.R.S.A., 1902; R.S.A., 1921; R.S.W. Member of New English Art Club. **£35 (w).**

CALDWALL, JOHN (died 1819). Born, Scotland, where he practised with much reputation as miniature painter. Brother of James Caldwall, b. London, 1739, English designer and engraver.

CAMERON, SIR DAVID YOUNG (1865-1945). Born, Glasgow; attended evening classes at Glasgow School of Art and from 1885 the Royal Institution, Edinburgh; took up etching (influenced by Meryon) and was successful in exhibitions throughout Europe; oils and watercolours of Scottish scenes; exhibited often with Glasgow School; knighted 1924. R.A.; R.S.A.; R.W.S. Died, Perth. **£280-750, 80-210 (w).**

CAMERON, DUNCAN (*fl.* 1850-1900). Prolific painter in oil of extensive Scottish landscapes; colours usually somewhat muddied in appearance. Exhibited R.S.A., 1863-1907. **£100-220, 18 (w).**

CAMERON, HUGH (1835-1918). Born, Edinburgh; architect's apprentice; Trustees' Academy; R.S.A. Schools; in London, 1876 to 1888; on Riviera about 1880; painted portraits and a few French peasant subjects, but chiefly scenes of humble Scottish and child life. A.R.S.A., 1859; R.S.A., 1869; R.S.W., 1878. Died, Edinburgh. **£105-230.**

CAMERON, KATHERINE (1874-1965). Born, Glasgow; sister of D. Y. Cameron (*q.v.*) and wife of art dealer and connoisseur, Arthur Kay; studied G.S.A. and Paris; much book illustration; worked in watercolour and gouache, also very competent etcher. R.S.W.; A.R.E., 1920; R.E., 1965. Died, Edinburgh. **£24-110 (w).**

CAMPBELL, THOMAS (1790-1858). Born, Edinburgh; apprenticed to marble cutter; studied at R. A. Schools, London; resided Italy, 1818-30; made busts and portrait statues. Died, London.

CAMPBELL, TOM (1865-1943). Born, Paisley; member of Glasgow Institute of Fine Art; painter of vividly coloured and very individual landscapes and seascapes. Died, Glasgow. **£35-240, 18-68 (w).**

CAMPION, GEORGE BRYANT (1796-1870). Painted landscapes in Scotland. Died, Woolwich. **£160-240 (w).**

CARMICHAEL, STEWART (1867-1950). One of the "Dundee School", active at the turn of the century; decorative work; a number of commissions for public buildings in Dundee. **£22, 10 (w).**

CARSE, ALEXANDER (died 1838). Genre painter, leading from David Allan to Wilkie; worked in London, 1812-20. Exhibited R.S.A., 1827-1836. **£700-750.**

CARSLAW, EVELYN (1881-1968). Studied G.S.A. and Paris; lived at Rhu and, latterly, Helensburgh; exhibited in Glasgow and West Helensburgh and District Art Club.

CASSIE, JAMES (1819-1879). Born, Inverurie; oils and watercolours, many of Aberdeen and district; also portraits and genre paintings; in later years his subjects taken almost exclusively from the sea and seashore. A.R.S.A., 1869; R.S.A., 1879. Died, Edinburgh. **£220.**

CAW, SIR JAMES LEWIS (1864-1950). Born, Ayr; studied G.S.A. and in Edinburgh; curator, Scottish National Portrait Gallery, 1895-1907, and 1907-1930 first Director of the National Galleries of Scotland; author of *Scottish Painting Past and Present* (1908). H.R.S.A. Died, Lasswade.

CHALMERS, GEORGE (died 1791). Born, Edinburgh; pupil of Allan Ramsay and later studied at Rome; resided for some years in Hull; painted portraits; exhibited at R.A., 1775-90. Died, London.

CHALMERS, GEORGE PAUL (1836-1878). Born, Montrose; apprenticed to ship chandler; worked under R. Scott Lauder, Trustees' Academy; painted portraits, genre and landscape subjects. A.R.S.A., 1867; R.S.A., 1871. Died, Edinburgh. **£35-145.**

CHALMERS, HECTOR (fl. 1880-1900). Painter of landscapes and coastal subjects, mainly on the east coast of Scotland. **£20-50.**

CHRISTIE, ALEXANDER (1807-1860). Born, Edinburgh; began as lawyer, but studied art under Sir W. Allan; Director of Trustees' Academy, 1845. A.R.S.A., 1848. Died, Edinburgh.

CHRISTIE, JAMES ELDER (1847-1914). Born, Guardbridge, Fifeshire; studied, Paisley and after 1874 at S. Kensington and R.A. Schools; from 1882-85 worked in Paris; removed to Glasgow and painted poetical and allegorical subjects. Died, London. **£26-280.**

CLARK, THOMAS (1820-1876). Lived and worked in Edinburgh; exhibited R.S.A., 1842-1880; landscapes throughout Scotland, the Borders and the Lake District. A.R.S.A., 1865.

CLERK, JOHN (1728-1812). Known as Clerk of Eldin. Born, Penicuik; etcher; said to have been taught by Paul Sandby, R.A.; married a sister of the Adam brothers; his son became Lord Eldin.

CORDINER, CHARLES (1746-1794). Studied at the Foulis Academy, 1763-66; lived at Banff where he was a minister; painted exquisite watercolours and published two illustrated topographical works *Antiquities and Scenery of the North of Scotland* (London, 1780) and *Remarkable Ruins and Romantic Prospects of North Britain* (London, 1795).

COVENTRY, ROBERT McGOWN (1855-1914). Born, Glasgow; studied at Glasgow School of Art and in Paris; lived in Glasgow, and travelled much abroad, but painted principally fishing and harbour scenes of east coast of Scotland. A.R.S.A., 1906. Died, Glasgow. **£130-360, 90 (w).**

COWIE, JAMES (1886-1956). Born, Monquhitter; studied G.S.A. from 1912 when he associated with McGlashan and Sivell (*q.v.*); powerful portraits with striking linear quality. A.R.S.A., 1936; R.S.A., 1943. **£10 (w).**

COWIESON, ANNIE M. (*fl.* 1880-1910). Painter of landscapes and seascapes; Caw in *Scottish Painting* refers to her ability in painting cats. Exhibited R.S.A., 1882-1912.

CRANSTOUN, JAMES H. (*fl.* 1840-1890). Associated with pictures of Perthshire. Exhibited R.S.A., 1844-1898. **£140-420.**

CRAWFORD, EDMUND THORNTON (1806-1885). Born, nr. Dalkeith; apprenticed to a house-painter, Edinburgh; studied at Trustees' Academy; from 1833 worked frequently in Holland; painted landscapes and seascapes. A.R.S.A., 1839; R.S.A., 1848. Died, Lasswade. **£55-1,050.**

CRAWFORD, WILLIAM CALDWELL (1879-1960). Born, Dalkeith; studied Edinburgh and Paris; a contemporary of James Riddell (*q.v.*) and Campbell Mitchell (*q.v.*); painted landscapes and exhibited regularly R.S.A. and S.S.A.; President S.S.A., 1928-30, and active member Scottish Arts Club.

CRAWFORD, WILLIAM (1825-1869). Lived and worked in Edinburgh; exhibited R.S.A. from 1841; specialised almost exclusively in portraiture. A.R.S.A., 1860.

CRAWHALL, JOSEPH (1861-1913). Born, Morpeth; his father, a close friend of Charles Keene; his mother, Scottish; associated with E. A. Walton and J. Guthrie (*q.v.*) in beginnings of Glasgow School; painted birds and animal subjects in watercolour; latterly, lived, hunted and painted in Yorkshire. **£20-48 (d).**

CROZIER, WILLIAM (1897-1930). Born, Edinburgh; studied Edinburgh College of Art and R.S.A. School; travelled extensively in France and Italy; exhibited R.S.A., 1920-1930; A.R.S.A., 1930. **£105.**

CUMMING, WILLIAM SKEOCH (1864-1929). Born, Edinburgh; studied at School of Art and R.S.A. School; worked in watercolour; painted portraits and military subjects; designer for tapestries woven in Lord Bute's studios at Corstorphine.

CURSITER, STANLEY (1887-1976). Born, Kirkwall; studied Edinburgh School of Art; returned Edinburgh after First World War; President S.S.A. and Keeper at the National Gallery of Scotland; 1948, appointed King's Painter and Limner in Scotland; portraits and landscapes. A.R.S.A., 1927; R.S.A., 1937. **£28-460.**

DALGLISH, WILLIAM (1860-1909). Glasgow artist in traditional mould. **£100.**

DAVIDSON, GEORGE DUTCH (1879-1901). Born, Goole; lived in Dundee during his tragically short life; self-taught but influenced by other Dundee artists (e.g. Foggie, Duncan); decorative, symbolic, Celtic-style work produced 1898-1901; travelled to London, Antwerp and Florence. Died, Dundee.

DAVISON, JEREMIAH (c. 1695-1745). Born in England of Scots parents; pupil of Lely; had large practice as portrait painter both in Edinburgh and London; noted for painting texture of satin.

DOBSON, HENRY J. (1858-1928). Born, Innerleithen, Peeblesshire; studied 1880 at School of Design, R. Institution, and R.S.A. Life School; painted interiors and genre. R.S.W., 1890.

DOCHARTY, ALEXANDER BROWNLIE (1862-1940). Born, Glasgow; notable for his extensive landscapes in oil of the Scottish Highlands; nephew of James Docharty (q.v.). Died, Glasgow. **£160-300.**

DOCHARTY, JAMES (1829-1878). Born, Bonhill, Dunbartonshire; son of calico block-cutter, worked as pattern designer; studied at Glasgow School of Art; painted mainly landscapes of Scottish Highlands. A.R.S.A., 1876. Died, Egypt. **£24-100.**

DONALD, JOHN MILNE (1817-1866). Born, Nairn; apprenticed to house-painter in Glasgow; worked, London, in shop of picture restorer; returned to Glasgow and painted Scottish landscape. Died, Glasgow.

DOUGLAS, ANDREW (1861-1935). Born, Midlothian; studied R.S.A. Life Class and visited Belgium, Holland and France followed by an extensive tour in America; fond of painting cattle in a Highland setting. A.R.S.A., 1920; R.S.A., 1932. **£24-130.**

DOUGLAS, JAMES (fl. 1860-1900). Edinburgh artist; exhibited R.S.A., 1861-1900. **£38 (w).**

DOUGLAS, JOHN (born 1867). Born, Kilmarnock; studied at G.S.A.; exhibited R.S.A.; R.S.W.; S.S.A.; and Glasgow Institute; lived in Ayr for many years.

DOUGLAS-IRVINE, LUCY CHRISTINA (born 1874). Born, Virginia Water, Surrey; Studied at Clifton, G.S.A. and Kemp-Welch School of Painting; exhibited R.S.W.; lived at Pittenweem.

DOUGLAS, Sir WILLIAM FETTES (1822-1891). Born, Edinburgh; from Royal High School entered Commercial Bank for 10 years, also pursuing study of art; painted figure subjects, showing his profound knowledge as historian and antiquary; later, excelled as painter in watercolour. A.R.S.A., 1851; R.S.A., 1854; P.R.S.A., 1882; Curator, N.G. of Scotland, 1877-82. Died, Newburgh, Fife. **£90.**

DOW, THOMAS MILLIE (1848-1919). Born, Dysart, Fifeshire; abandoned law for art; studied at Ecole des Beaux-Arts, Paris, and under Carolus Duran; painted landscapes in oil and watercolour. ˙R.S.W., 1885. Died, St Ives, Cornwall. **£96-320.**

DOWELL, CHARLES R. (*fl.* 1920s). Glasgow painter of street scenes, portraits and interiors; exhibited at the Glasgow Institute; R.S.W., 1933. **£10-25.**

DOWNIE, JOHN P. (1871-1945). Born, Glasgow; worked there and on the Continent.

DOWNIE, PATRICK (1854-1945). Born, Greenock; studied in Paris; exhibited R.A.; R.I.; Suffolk Street; R.S.A.; R.S.W.; and Glasgow Institute; gold medal at the Paris Salon, 1901; maritime subjects with many views of the Clyde; R.S.W. **£70-310, 126 (w).**

DRUMMOND, JAMES (1816-1877). Born, Edinburgh; studied at Trustees' Academy; steeped in Scottish history and archaeology. A.R.A., 1845; R.S.A., 1852; Curator of National Gallery of Scotland, 1868-77. Died, Edinburgh. **£320.**

DUNCAN, JOHN (1866-1945). Born, Dundee; studied Dundee College of Art and later in Belgium, Germany and Italy; 1901-1904 Associate Professor of Art, University of Chicago; highly decorative work, often ecclesiastical in theme; favourite medium, tempera. A.R.S.A., 1910; R.S.A.; R.S.W.

DUNCAN, THOMAS (1807-1845). Born, Kinclaven, Perthshire; studied at Trustees' Academy, Edinburgh; painted historical subjects and portraits; became one of original members of R.S.A., 1826; A.R.A., 1843. Died, Edinburgh.

DYCE, WILLIAM (1806-1864). Born, Aberdeen; graduated M.A. at Marischal College; studied art, Edinburgh and London; in Rome, 1825 and 1827-29, studying fresco; worked in Edinburgh; appointed Secretary of School of Design, Somerset House, London, 1839; painted frescoes in Houses of Parliament; also figure, portrait and landscape subjects, and designs for stained glass. A.R.A., 1844; R.A., 1848; H.R.S.A., 1854. Died, Streatham, Surrey.

EWBANK, JOHN WILSON (1799-1847). Born, Gateshead; painter of landscapes and seascapes. R.S.A., 1826. Died, Edinburgh. **£70-600.**

FAED, JAMES (1821-1911). Born, Barlay Mill, Kirkcudbrightshire; brother to the famous painters, James became renowned for his mezzotint engraving; reproduced many of his brothers' pictures as well as those of artists such as Sir Frances Grant (*q.v.*) and Sir George Reid (*q.v.*).

FAED, JOHN (1820-1902). Born at Barlay Mill, Kirkcudbrightshire, elder brother of Thomas Faed, R.A.; at age of 12 travelled through Galloway painting miniature portraits; eight years later studied at Trustees' Academy, Edinburgh. A.R.S.A., 1847; R.S.A., 1851. Worked, London, 1862-80, exhibiting at R.A. Died, Gatehouse-of-Fleet. **£600.**

FAED, THOMAS (1826-1900). Born, Barlay Mill, Kirk-cudbrightshire; pupil of his brother John (*q.v.*); studied at School of Design, Edinburgh, settled London, 1852; painted pathetic and sentimental sides of Scottish domestic life. A.R.S.A., 1849; A.R.A., 1861; R.A., 1864. Died, London. **£380, 50 (w).**

FARQUHARSON, DAVID (1839-1907). Born Blair-gowrie, Perthshire; began as apprentice decorator; moved to Edinburgh, 1872; worked as landscape painter, from 1886-94 in London, thereafter at Sennen Cove, Land's End. A.R.S.A., 1882; A.R.A., 1905. Died, Birnam, Perthshire. **£70-600, 45 (w).**

FARQUHARSON, JOSEPH (1845-1935). Born, Edinburgh; taught by P. Graham, and exhibited at R.S.A. at age 13; studied in R.S.A. Life Class and at Paris; painted Highland landscapes. A.R.A., 1900; R.A., 1915. **£75-200, 2,400 (1975).**

FENWICK, THOMAS (?-1850). Newcastle artist; much painting in Scotland; exhibited R.S.A., 1835-1850. **£1,100 (1975).**

FERGUSON, WILLIAM GOUW (1632-1695?). Born, and received early training, in Scotland; resided in Italy, at the Hague, 1660-68, at Amsterdam, 1681. Painted dead game and still life subjects, in Dutch manner.

FERGUSSON, JOHN DUNCAN (1874-1961). Born, Leith; abandoned medicine for art and settled in Paris in 1905; painting developed Fauvist tendencies under influence of Picasso, Segonzac and Derain; with 1914 war

JOHN KNOX (1778-1845)
The Govan Ferry
Sold by Sotheby's in Scotland
£7,600

CHARLES LEES (1800-1880)
Lunch on the Moors
Sold by Sotheby's in Scotland
£5,500

he moved to London and painted for Admiralty; returned Paris between wars; founded New Art Club and the New Scottish Group in Glasgow. R.B.A. **£450-600, 48 (d).**

FERRIER, GEORGE STRATTON (died 1912). Exhibited London galleries from 1878; R.S.W.; R.E., 1881; R.I., 1898; painter of landscapes and etcher. **£22-45 (w).**

FILLANS, JAMES (1808-1852). Born, Wilsontown, Lanarkshire; apprenticed to a mason at Paisley; turned attention to sculpture; settled London, 1836; moved to Glasgow, 1852. Died, Glasgow.

FLEMING, JOHN (1792-1845). Born, and lived, in Greenock; specialised in the painting of landscapes.

FLINT, ROBERT PURVES (1883-1947). Born, Edinburgh; younger brother of Sir William Russell Flint (*q.v.*); landscapes and coast scenes in oil and watercolour; R.S.W., 1918; A.R.W.S., 1932; R.W.S., 1937.

FLINT, SIR WILLIAM RUSSELL (1880-1969). Born, Edinburgh; lived and painted in London and on the Continent for most of his life; most famous for his book illustrations and paintings of semi-nudes in Mediterranean settings; signed prints of these now command remarkably high prices. R.A.; P.R.W.S.; R.S.W.; R.O.I.; R.E.; N.S. Died, London. **£720-1,000 (w).**

FOGGIE, David (1878-1948). Born, Dundee; trained in Antwerp at age of 20, later in Paris, Florence and

Holland; contemporary of John Duncan, Alexander Grieve and Stewart Carmichael (*q.v.*); well known for portraits but also painted landscapes. A.R.S.A., 1925; R.S.A., 1930.

FORBES, ALEXANDER (1802-1839). Lived and worked in Edinburgh; exhibited R.S.A., 1828-1840; genre and animal pictures. A.R.S.A., 1830.

FORBES, ANN (1745-1834). Grand-daughter of William Aikman; studied, Rome, *c.* 1770; had large clientèle in Scotland for portraits in oil and watercolour, but mostly in crayon. Died, Edinburgh.

FRASER, ALEXANDER (1786-1865). Lived and worked in London but travelled extensively in Scotland; exhibited R.S.A., 1827-1863; genre and landscape. A.R.S.A., 1840; H.R.S.A., 1827-1840. **£60-320.**

FRASER, ALEXANDER (1828-1899). Born Woodcockdale, Linlithgow; studied at Edinburgh School of Design; encouraged by Sir W. Fettes Douglas (*q.v.*); painted figure subjects, and later entirely landscapes. A.R.S.A., 1858; R.S.A., 1862. Died, Musselburgh. **£70-600.**

FRAZER, WILLIAM MILLER (1864-1961). Born Scone; entered R.S.A. Schools *c.* 1882; exhibited at R.S.A. from 1884 and achieved a record by exhibiting for 73 consecutive years; landscapes in oil; President S.S.A., 1908; President Scottish Arts Club, 1926; A.R.S.A., 1909; R.S.A., 1924. Died, Edinburgh. **£65-380.**

FRENCH, ANNIE (1872-1965). Born, Glasgow; Mrs George Wooliscroft Read; taught G.S.A., 1909-1914;

exhibited London, Paris and Canada; most competent book illustrator; influence of Beardsley in her work. Died, Jersey, C.I. **£150 (w).**

FULTON, DAVID (1848-1930). Glasgow artist in traditional mould. R.S.W. **£48-180.**

GALLAWAY, ALEXANDER (worked *c.* 1794-1812; working in Glasgow, 1801, in Edinburgh, 1811-12). A miniature by him was shown at Portrait Exhibition, South Kensington, 1865.

GAMLEY, ANDREW ARCHER (*fl.* 1920-1950). Born, Johnshaven, Kincardineshire; studied at the R.S.A. and won the first Carnegie Scholarship; exhibited R.S.A.; R.S.W., Glasgow Institute and Liverpool; landscapes and coastal subjects in oil and watercolour; R.S.W., 1924. **£17-30 (w).**

GAULD, DAVID (1867-1936). Born, Glasgow; worked originally as lithographer, then on newspaper illustration and design for stained glass; became associated with Glasgow School; painted mainly landscape with buildings in twilight and also renowned for his cattle pictures. A.R.S.A., 1918; R.S.A., 1924. Died, Glasgow. **£260-420, 40 (w).**

GAVIN, ROBERT (1827-1883). Born, Leith; lived and worked in Edinburgh; travelled to North Africa; exhibited R.S.A., 1846-1882; portraits and genre pictures. A.R.S.A., 1854; R.S.A., 1879. Died, Newhaven. **£38-750.**

GEDDES, ANDREW (1783-1844). Born, Edinburgh; educated at Royal High School and Edinburgh University; went to London about 1807 and studied at R.A. Schools; travelled extensively on Continent, and worked as portrait painter, London and Edinburgh; with Wilkie, promoted revival of etching. A.R.A., 1832. Died, London. **£180-500.**

GEDDES, EWAN (died 1935). Exhibited in Scotland and at London galleries from 1891; R.S.W., 1902; lived Edinburgh; landscape paintings principally in watercolour. **£14-38 (w), 62.**

GEDDES, WILLIAM (*fl.* 1860-1880). Exhibited R.S.A., 1865-1884; landscapes and rural scenes. **£40-220.**

GEIKIE, WALTER (1795-1837). Born, Edinburgh; deaf and dumb; painted Scottish life from humorous and satirical aspect; draughtsman and etcher. A.R.S.A., 1831; R.S.A., 1834.

GIBB, ROBERT (1801-1837). Born, Dundee; foundation member of the Scottish Academy; painter of landscape in oils and watercolour. A.R.S.A., 1826; R.S.A., 1829.

GIBB, ROBERT (1845-1932). Born, Laurieston; studied at R.S.A. Schools; painted portraits and landscapes, but principally military themes. A.R.S.A., 1878; R.S.A., 1882. King's Limner for Scotland. Died, Edinburgh. **£300.**

GIBB, WILLIAM (1839-1929). Born, Laurieston; elder brother of R. Gibb, R.S.A.; trained as lithographer;

made reputation by watercolours and lithographs of relics, precious objects, etc. Died, London. **£15.**

GIBSON, PATRICK (1782-1829). Painter, etcher and writer on art; trained Edinburgh at Trustees' Academy and under Alexander Nasmyth. R.S.A., 1826. **£160.**

GIBSON, WILLIAM ALFRED (1868-1931). Born, Glasgow; abandoned business for art; Self-trained; painted landscapes, follower of modern Dutch and Barbizon Schools. Died, Glasgow. **£140-650.**

GILES, JAMES WILLIAM (1801-1870). Born, Glasgow; animal and landscape subjects in oil and watercolour; tour of Italy, 1824, and executed many drawings of landscape and antique sculpture. R.S.A., 1829. **£200-300.**

GILLIES, SIR WILLIAM GEORGE (1898-1973). Born, Haddington; studied Edinburgh College of Art 1916-1923, and then with Lhote in Paris and in Italy; taught at E.C.A. from 1926; Principal of College 1961-66. S.S.A., 1937; A.R.S.A., 1940; R.S.A., 1947; R.S.W., 1950; P.R.S.W., 1963; C.B.E., 1957; A.R.A., 1964. **£240, 60-220 (w).**

GLASS, JOHN (1820-1885). Lived and worked in Edinburgh; exhibited R.S.A. 1840-1886; painted ponies, horses and other animals. A.R.S.A., 1849.

GLASS, JOHN HAMILTON (*fl.* 1880-1910). Prolific painter of watercolours depicting Highland scenes, harbours of the Forth and views of Holland; also oils;

S.S.A.; lived and worked in Musselburgh. Exhibited R.S.A. from 1890. **£62-85, 18-35 (w).**

GLASS, WILLIAM MERVYN (1885-1965). Painter of coastal scenes and seascapes; signed pictures with initials W.M.G.; studied Aberdeen School of Art; R.S.A.; Paris and Italy; exhibited R.S.A.; R.A.; Glasgow Institute; A.R.S.A., 1934; R.S.A., 1959; President S.S.A., 1930-33. **£22-48.**

GORDON, JAMES (*fl.* 1820s). Active in Aberdeen area 1820s; pencil and wash impressions of local landmarks.

GORDON, SIR JOHN WATSON (1788-1864). Born, Edinburgh; son of Captain James Watson, R.N.; studied at Trustees' Academy; painted historical subjects, and thereafter portraits only; assumed name of Gordon, 1826. R.S.A., 1829; P.R.S.A., 1850; A.R.A., 1841; R.A., 1851. King's Limner for Scotland, and knighted, 1850. Died, Edinburgh. **£100-270.**

GOWANS, GEORGE RUSSELL (1843-1924). Born, Aberdeen; drawings, watercolours and oils of Aberdeen and area; R.S.W.

GRAHAM, PETER (1836-1921). Born, Edinburgh; studied at Trustees' Academy under Scott Lauder (*q.v.*); removed to London, 1866; painted sea-coast scenery and landscapes with cattle. A.R.A., 1877; R.A., 1881. Died, London. **£200.**

GRAHAM, ROBERT B. (*fl.* 1850-1880). Exhibited R.S.A., 1857-1878.

GRAHAM, THOMAS (1840-1906). Born, Kirkwall; studied at Trustees' Academy under Scott Lauder, with Orchardson and Pettie; with these two settled in same house in London; painted portraits, and figure subjects with seafaring incident. H.R.S.A., 1883. Died, Edinburgh.

GRAHAM-GILBERT, JOHN (1794-1866). Born, Glasgow; assumed name of Gilbert on marriage; R.A. Schools, London, 1818; studied some years in Italy; settled in Edinburgh as portrait painter; moved in 1834 to Glasgow. R.S.A., 1829. Died, Glasgow.

GRANT, FRANCIS (1803-1878). Born, Kilgraston, Perthshire; gave up legal profession for art; painted hunting scenes, then entirely portraits. A.R.A., 1842; R.A., 1851; P.R.A., 1866. **£60 (1975).**

GRANT, THOMAS F. (*fl.* 1860-1880). Painter of Highland scenes; exhibited R.S.A., 1868-1879.

GRAY, NORAH NEILSON (1882-1931). Born, Helensburgh; studied G.S.A. under Newberry (*q.v.*); 1906 joined G.S.A. staff; lived and worked in Glasgow; exhibited in Paris with considerable success; imaginative and highly decorative work; outstanding child portraiture. Died, Glasgow. **Pair: £165.**

GRIEVE, ALEC (1864-1933). One of the "Dundee School", active at the turn of the century.

GRIEVE, WALTER GRAHAM (1872-1937). Born, Kirkliston, West Lothian; studied at Royal Institution and at R.S.A. Life School, 1896-99; began career as lithographer; Art Adviser to Thos. Nelson & Son; painted many striking pictures of groups of people in unusual situations. A.R.S.A., 1920; R.S.A., 1929; R.S.W., 1934. Died, Edinburgh.

GUNN, SIR HERBERT JAMES (1893-1964).   Born, Glasgow; studied G.S.A. and Academie Julien, Paris, under Jean-Paul Laurens; portraits, landscape and still-life in oil and watercolour.   R.P., 1945; A.R.A., 1953; P.R.P., 1953; R.A., 1961; knighted, 1963. **£26.**

GUTHRIE, SIR JAMES (1859-1930).   Born, Greenock; graduated M.A., Glasgow; abandoned law for painting; studied in London with some help from John Pettie, R.A., and in Paris; identified with Glasgow School movement; painted figure subjects in landscape, and later entirely portraits.   A.R.S.A., 1888; R.S.A., 1892; P.R.S.A., 1902-19; knighted, 1902.   Died, Rhu, Dunbartonshire. **£700.**

HALL, GEORGE WRIGHT (1895-1974).   Born, Edinburgh; studied R.S.A. School and Edinburgh College of Art; exhibited R.A.; R.S.A.; R.S.W.; S.S.A.; painter in oil and watercolour with many fine portraits; at the time of his death he was Director, Edinburgh Art Centre. Died, Edinburgh.

HALSWELLE, KEELEY (1832-1891). Born, Richmond; lived and worked in Edinburgh, 1856-1872, thereafter in

London; exhibited R.S.A., 1856-1891; landscapes and historical studies. A.R.S.A., 1865. Died, Paris.

HAMILTON, GAVIN (1723-1798). Born, Lanark; studied under Masucci; worked at Rome; painted portraits. Died, Rome.

HAMILTON, JAMES (c. 1640-c. 1720). Born, Murdieston, Fife; settled in Brussels, and later in Germany; painted still life and flowers.

HAMILTON, JAMES WHITELAW (1861-1932). Born, Glasgow; studied in Glasgow, Paris, Munich; painted landscape in oil and watercolour. R.S.W., 1895; A.R.S.A., 1911; R.S.A., 1922. Died, Helensburgh. **£35.**

HAMILTON, MAGGIE (1867-1952). Born, Glasgow; younger sister of J. Whitelaw Hamilton (q.v.); 1897 married A. N. Paterson, younger brother of James Paterson (q.v.); fine embroideress. Died, Helensburgh.

HANSEN, HANS (1853-1947). Studied painting Edinburgh; exhibited R.A.; R.I.; and R.B.A., from 1876; silver medal at Salzburg International Exhibition; R.S.W. **£20-48 (w).**

HARDIE, CHARLES MARTIN (1858-1916). Born, East Linton; studied at R.S.A. Schools; painted portraits, landscape, genre. A.R.S.A., 1886; R.S.A., 1895. Died, Edinburgh. **£50-380.**

HARGITT, EDWARD (1835-1895). Born, Edinburgh; landscape painter. **£13-20 (w).**

HARVEY, GEORGE (1806-1876). Born, St Ninians, near Stirling; became bookseller's apprentice; studied at Trustees' Academy, Edinburgh; painted Scottish religious history and life, historical subjects, and landscapes. P.R.S.A., 1864; knighted, 1867. **£100, 280 (1975).**

HAY, GEORGE (1831-1912). Born, Edinburgh; lived and worked in Edinburgh; exhibited R.S.A., 1856-1913; historical scenes. A.R.S.A., 1869; R.S.A., 1876.

HAY, THOMAS MARJORIBANKS (1862-1921). Began as designer for stained glass; studied painting at R.S.A. Schools; painted landscapes in watercolour. Died, Edinburgh. **£5-88 (w).**

HENDERSON, JOHN (1860-1924). Born, Glasgow; "a refined feeling for woodland and burnside landscape and a cultured ideal of design, in which balance of mass and rhythm of line are combined with respect for those tender and characteristic beauties of natural form and growth which charm one so in nature" (Caw: *Scottish Painting).* **£110.**

HENDERSON, JOSEPH (1832-1908). Born, Stanley, Perthshire; studied at Trustees' Academy, Edinburgh; settled in Glasgow; painted marine subjects and portraits; worked in oil and watercolour; foundation member of R.S.W., 1878. Died, Ballantrae. **£80-320.**

HENDERSON, JOSEPH MORRIS (1864-1936). Born, Glasgow, son of Joseph Henderson, R.S.W.; graduate, Glasgow University; studied at Glasgow School of Art;

painted landscape and seaside subjects. A.R.S.A., 1928; R.S.A., 1935. Died, Glasgow. **£90-110.**

HENRY, GEORGE F. (1858-1943). Born, Irvine; attended G.S.A., 1822 and became involved with Glasgow School; close friend of E. A. Hornel and went with him in 1893 to Japan; important influence in Glasgow School; landscapes, portraits and figure subjects in oil and water-colour. A.R.S.A., 1892; R.S.W., 1900; R.S.A., 1902; A.R.A., 1907; R.A., 1920. Died, London. **£650, 320 (w).**

HERALD, JAMES WATTERSTON (1859-1914). Born, Forfar; largely self-taught, but watercolour work influenced later by Arthur Melville; spent 10 years in London; from 1901 lived in retirement at Arbroath; produced many fine harbour and sea paintings. **£42-240 (p).**

HERDMAN, ROBERT (1829-1888). Born, Rattray, Perthshire; studied at Trustees' Academy, Edinburgh; painted incidents in Scottish history and portraits. A.R.S.A., 1858; R.S.A., 1863. **£45.**

HERDMAN, ROBERT DUDDINGSTONE (1863-1922). Son of Robert Herdman, R.S.A. (*q.v.*); studied R.S.A. Schools and Paris; travelled Spain and Holland; exhibited London, Paris, Munich, Vienna and Edinburgh; portraits and genre paintings. A.R.S.A., 1908; S.S.A. **£300.**

HERON, JAMES. Exhibited R.S.A. from 1873; mainly watercolours but some oils; landscapes and pastoral subjects treated traditionally. **£10-35 (w).**

HILL, DAVID OCTAVIUS (1802-1870). Born, Perth; studied at Trustees' Academy, Edinburgh; painted landscapes and illustrated Burns, etc.; for several years worked at "Signing the Deed of Demission. . . ." containing 470 portraits of leaders of the Free Church of Scotland; pioneer in photography. Foundation associate of R.S.A., 1826; member, 1829; Secretary, 1830-69. Died, Edinburgh. **£380-700.**

HISLOP, ANDREW HEALEY (1887-1954). Studied Edinburgh College of Art and, later, British School in Rome; exhibited R.S.A., R.A., G.I., etc.; taught E.C.A. and lived in Edinburgh; S.S.A. **£18-24.**

HOLE, WILLIAM (1846-1917). Born, Salisbury; studied in Trustees' School and R.S.A. Life Class; painted mural decorations, etc., well known for his reproductive etchings. A.R.S.A., 1878; R.S.A., 1889. Died, Edinburgh. **£22 (d), 400 (1975).**

HOPE, ROBERT (1868-1936). Born, Edinburgh; worked as lithographic draughtsman and book illustrator; studied at School of Design and R.S.A. Life School, and in Paris; painted landscape and figures, portraits and decorative schemes. A.R.S.A., 1911; R.S.A., 1925. Died, Edinburgh. **£42-200.**

HORNEL, EDWARD ATKINSON (1864-1933). Born of Scottish parents. Bacchus Marsh, N.S.W., Australia; brought to Britain, 1866, and settled in Kirkcudbright; studied at Trustees' Academy, Edinburgh, and at Antwerp; identified himself with Glasgow School; worked in Japan, 1893-94; painted children in flower-decked woods or at seaside. Died, Kirkcudbright. **£1,500-3,400.**

HOUSTON, GEORGE (1869-1947). Born, Dalry; lithographer and etcher with *Glasgow Evening Citizen* in 1898; exhibited at R.S.A., from 1898; landscape, still life and interiors in oil, watercolour and pastel. A.R.S.A., 1909; R.S.A., 1924; R.S.W. Died, Dalry. **£70-700, 24-52 (w).**

HOUSTON, JOHN ADAM P. (1812-1884). Born, Gwydyr Castle; landscape painter. A.R.S.A., 1842; R.S.A., 1845. Died, London. **£460 (1975).**

HOUSTON, JOHN RENNIE McKENZIE (1856-1932). Born, Glasgow; R.S.W. Died. Rutherglen. **£50.**

HOUSTON, ROBERT (1891-1940). Born, Ayrshire; painted on west coast of Scotland; R.S.W. **£90.**

HOWE, JAMES (1780-1836). Born, Skirling; animal studies and panoramas. Died, Newhaven.

HUNT, THOMAS (1853-1929). Born, Yorkshire; came to Scotland 1878 and worked at G.S.A.; drew his subjects from the Highlands; A.R.S.A., 1925; R.S.W. Died, Glasgow. **£10-120 (w).**

HUNTER, COLIN (1841-1904). Born, Glasgow; began life a clerk; encouraged by Milne Donald to take up art; settled finally in London; painted seashore and fishing subjects. A.R.A., 1884; R.S.W., 1879. Died, Kensington. **£120-300.**

HUNTER, GEORGE LESLIE (1877-1931). Born, Rothesay, Isle of Bute; studied in San Francisco, Paris,

London; settled in Glasgow; painted landscapes and still life. Died, Glasgow. **£190-1,100.**

HUNTER, MASON (1854-1921). Born, Glasgow; lived and worked in Edinburgh; exhibited R.S.A., 1879-1916; landscapes and seascapes. A.R.S.A., 1913. **£40.**

HURT, LOUIS BOSWORTH (1856-1929). Born, Ashbourne; painted in Scotland; favourite subject: Highland cattle and undoubtedly king of the cattle painters. Died, Matlock, 1929. **£60-1,100.**

HUTCHESON, WALTER (*Fl.* 1870-1890). Exhibited R.S.A., 1869-1890; genre paintings.

HUTCHISON, ROBERT GEMMELL (1855-1936). Born, Edinburgh; worked as seal engraver; studied at Art School of the Board of Manufacturers, Edin.; painted in oil, watercolour, pastel, subjects of landscape, interiors and portraits. A.R.S.A., 1901; R.S.A., 1911; R.S.W., 1895; R.O.I. **£350-2,950.**

HUTCHISON, SIR WILLIAM OLIPHANT (1889-1970). Born, Kirkcaldy; studied Paris and later Edinburgh College of Art under E. A. Walton (*q.v.*) whose youngest daughter, Margery, he married; Director, G.S.A., 1933-1943; portraits. A.R.S.A., 1937; R.S.A., 1943; P.R.S.A., 1950-1959.

IRVINE, JAMES (1824-1889). Born, Forfarshire; distinguished and popular portrait painter; exhibited R.S.A.

IRVINE, JOHN (1805-1888). Lived and worked in Edinburgh, 1843-1858; exhibited R.S.A., 1827-1862; specialised in portraits. A.R.S.A., 1834.

JAMESONE, GEORGE (1586-1644). Born, Aberdeen; apprentice to John Anderson, an Edinburgh artist; commenced as portrait painter in Aberdeen, and later in Edinburgh; known as "The Scottish Van Dyck". Died, Edinburgh.

JAMIESON, ALEXANDER (1873-1937). Born, Glasgow; painted in Scotland and travelled extensively on the Continent later; his later oils display a well-developed, personalised style; landscapes, portraits and decorative works. Died, London. **£55-200.**

JENNINGS-BROWN, H. W. (*Fl.* 1870-1890). Dundee painter; exhibited R.S.A., 1869-1887.

JOHNSTONE, GEORGE WHITTON (1849-1901). Born, Glamis; lived and worked in Edinburgh; exhibited R.S.A., 1872-1901; landscapes and seascapes. A.R.S.A., 1883; R.S.A., 1895. Died, Edinburgh. **£38-65.**

KAY, ARCHIBALD (1860-1935). Born, Glasgow; studied at Glasgow School of Art and in Paris; painted Highland landscape. A.R.S.A., 1916; R.S.A., 1930; V.P.R.S.W. Died, Glasgow. **£20-220.**

KAY, JAMES (1858-1942). Born, Lamlash; studied at G.S.A.; exhibited at R.A. from 1889 and in many exhibitions abroad, e.g. Paris 1894, Brussels 1895, Rouen 1906; landscapes, seascapes, portraits and figure subjects in all media; highly developed style. A.R.S.A., 1933; R.S.A., 1938; R.S.W. Died, Whistlefield. **£50-420, 70-270 (w).**

KAY, JOHN (1742-1826). Born, Dalkeith; trained as a barber but developed remarkable skill in drawing and etching; hundreds of etchings and caricatures, also extremely competent miniature painter; fine self-portrait in oil extant. Died, Edinburgh.

KENNEDY, WILLIAM (1859-1918). Born, Paisley; studied in Paris; after 1885, attached to Glasgow School, painted military subjects, camps, canteens, etc.; later, rural life and landscape, chiefly in Berkshire. **£115-190.**

KEPPIE, JOHN (1863-1945). Born, Glasgow; studied Glasgow University and Atelier Pascal, Paris; senior partner in Glasgow architects firm Keppie and Henderson and was joined there by Charles Rennie Mackintosh (*q.v.*); competent water-colourist. A.R.S.A., 1920; R.S.A., 1937; P.R.I.B.A. Died, Ayrshire.

KERR, HENRY WRIGHT (1857-1936). Born, Edinburgh; worked in commercial firm at Leith; studied in R.S.A. Life Class; painted character studies in water-colour and, later, portraits in oil. A.R.S.A., 1893; R.S.A., 1909; R.S.W., 1891. Died, Edinburgh. **£15-75 (w).**

KIDD, JOSEPH BARTHOLOMEW (1808-1889). Lived and worked in Edinburgh; exhibited R.S.A., 1827-1836;

SIR JOSEPH NOEL PATON (1821-1901)
Thomas the Rhymer and the Queen of the Faeries
Sold by Sotheby's in Scotland
£3,600

ARTHUR MELVILLE (1830-1923)
The Orange Market, Saragossa
(watercolour)
Sold by Sotheby's in Scotland
£1,000

landscapes and seascapes. A.R.S.A., 1826; R.S.A., 1829-1858.

KING, JESSIE MARION (1875-1949). Born, New Kilpatrick; studied G.S.A. and won travelling scholarship to Italy and Germany; splendid and much sought-after book illustrator; also designed jewellery, wallpapers and fabrics; 1908 married painter and critic Ernest Taylor; lived in Salford, Paris and Kirkcudbright. Died, Kirkcudbright. **£160 (w).**

KNOX, JOHN (1778-1845). Born, Paisley; lived and worked in Glasgow; exhibited R.A., 1828-1835; travelled on the Continent; painted landscapes and views of Glasgow, notably extensive panoramas; taught Horatio McCulloch (*q.v.*) and Daniel MacNee (*q.v.*). **£600.**

LAIDLAW, NICOL (born 1886). Born, Edinburgh; studied Edinburgh College of Art; exhibited R.A. and R.S.A.; painter and etcher of portraits and landscapes. **£14-48.**

LAING, FRANK (1852-1907). One of the "Dundee School", active at the turn of the century. **£10.**

LAING, JAMES GARDEN (1852-1915). Born, Aberdeen; served apprenticeship as architect; studied art in Glasgow. R.S.W., 1885. Died, Glasgow. **£50 (w).**

LAMOND, WILLIAM B. (1857-1924). Born, Newtyle; lived in Dundee from 1864; popular at first as portrait

painter and then moved on to landscapes and seascapes.
R.B.A. Died, Dundee. **£29-420.**

LAUDER, CHARLES JAMES (?-1920). Studied at
Glasgow School of Design; exhibited in London galleries
from 1890; exhibited R.S.A., 1872-1900; painted in Italy
and along the Thames returning to Scotland late in life.
R.S.W.; R.G.I. Died, Glasgow. **£76 (w).**

LAUDER, JAMES ECKFORD (1811-1869). Born, Edinburgh; studied at Trustees' Academy; spent four years in
Rome; instructed by his brother, R. S. Lauder; painted
figure subjects and landscapes. A.R.S.A., 1839; R.S.A.,
1846. Died, Edinburgh.

LAUDER, ROBERT SCOTT (1803-1869). Born,
Edinburgh; studied at Trustees' Academy; worked three
years in London; from 1833 to 1838; studied at Rome,
Florence, Bologna, Venice; settled in London, 1838;
painted sacred subjects and incidents from Scott's novels;
elected Master of Trustees' Academy, Edinburgh, 1852,
and had great influence on Scottish art; Orchardson,
Pettie, Chalmers, McTaggart were his pupils. R.S.A.,
1879. Died, Edinburgh.

LAVERY, SIR JOHN (1856-1941). Born, Belfast;
studied art in Glasgow, London and Paris; influenced by
Bastien-Lepage and, later, Manet and Whistler; central
figure in the Glasgow School; very fine portraits in oil.
A.R.S.A., 1892, R.S.A., 1896; R.A.; R.H.A. Died,
Kilmanganny. **£35-260.**

LAW, ANDREW (1873-1967). Born, Kilmaurs; studied
G.S.A. under Fra Newberry (*q.v.*) and in Paris; exhibited

R.S.A., G.I., Paris Salon; staff of G.S.A. for 20 years; painted portraits, animals and street scenes. **£10-100.**

LE CONTE, JOHN (*fl.* 1860-1880). Exhibited R.S.A.; well-drawn watercolours of Edinburgh street scenes. **£20-38 (w).**

LEES, CHARLES (1800-1880). Lived and worked in Edinburgh; exhibited R.S.A., 1829-1880; landscapes and portraits. A.R.S.A., 1829; R.S.A., 1829.

LEGGATT, ALEXANDER (*Fl.* 1850-1880). Exhibited R.S.A. **£340.**

LEITCH, WILLIAM LEIGHTON (1804-1883). Born, Glasgow; removed to Cumnock, and decorated snuff boxes; went to London and became scene painter; travelled in Italy for four years; taught watercolour to Queen Victoria and Royal Family. V.P.R.I., 1863-83. Died, London.

LEYDE, OTTO THEODORE (1835-1897). Born, Wehlan (Germany); resided and painted for many years in Edinburgh; genre paintings and landscapes. A.R.S.A., 1870; R.S.A., 1880; R.S.W. Died Edinburgh. **£95, 64 (w).**

LINTOTT, HENRY (1877-1965). Born, Brighton; studied at Royal College of Art and taught at Edinburgh College of Art from 1902; Memorial Exhibition at R.S.A., 1965; A.R.S.A., 1916; R.S.A., 1923. Died, Edinburgh. **£10-20 (w).**

LIZARS, WILLIAM HOME (1788-1859). Born, Edinburgh; educated at Royal High School, and apprenticed to his father, an engraver; painted portraits and subject-pictures; abandoned painting in 1812 to succeed to his father's business. Died, Jedburgh.

LOCHHEAD, JOHN (1866-1921). Born, Glasgow; landscapes; R.B.A. **£260 (1975).**

LOCKHART, WILLIAM EWART (1846-1900). Born, Dumfriesshire; studied art at Trustees' Academy, Edinburgh; later settled in London; in 1887 painted "Jubilee Celebration in Westminster Abbey" for Queen Victoria; also painted portraits, landscapes, genre. A.R.S.A., 1870; R.S.A., 1873. Died, London. **With J. B. Macdonald: £72.**

LORIMER, JOHN HENRY (1856-1936). Educated at Edinburgh Academy and Edinburgh University, then R.S.A. Schools; worked on Continent and, in 1884, under Carolus Duran, Paris; painted landscapes, flower pieces, subject-pictures, portraits; A.R.S.A., R.S.A., 1900. Died, Pittenweem.

LUMSDEN, ERNEST STEPHEN (1883-1948). Born, London; trained Reading Art College and, later, Paris and Spain; taught Edinburgh College of Art; expert in etching and author of standard work *Art of Etching* (1925). A.R.S.A., 1923; R.S.A., 1933. Died, Edinburgh.

LYON, THOMAS BONAR (born 1873). Studied G.S.A. and later in France, Belgium and Holland; exhibited R.S.A. and Paris Salon; lived in Ayr and painted many landscapes of the Ayrshire coast in oil and watercolour. **£18-40.**

McADAM, WALTER (1866-1935). Born, Glasgow; painter Scottish landscapes and rural scenes. Died, Glasgow. **£80.**

MACALLUM, HAMILTON (1841-1896). Born, Bute; studied R.A.; associated with paintings of the sea in oil and watercolour. R.I.

MacBETH, NORMAN (1821-1888). Exhibited R.S.A., 1846-1888; specialised in portraiture. A.R.S.A., 1870; R.S.A., 1880.

MacBETH, ROBERT WALKER (1848-1910). Born, Glasgow, son of N. Macbeth, R.S.A.; went to London, illustrator to *Graphic*; painted landscapes and figures. A.R.A., 1883; R.A., 1903; R.W.S.; R.E.

McBEY, JAMES (1883-1959). Born Newburgh; began work in a bank, studying art in spare time, and became known as an etcher; official war artist with Egyptian Expeditionary Force 1917; travelled extensively in Holland, France, Spain, Italy and North Africa; U.S. citizen in 1942; etchings and watercolours. R.E. Died, Tangiers. **£200, 34-105 (w).**

MACBRIDE, ALEXANDER (1859-1955). Born, Glasgow; studied G.S.A. and Paris (Academie Julien); exhibited in Scotland and R.I.; landscapes in watercolour. R.S.W.; R.I. Died, Cathcart.

McCANCE, WILLIAM (1894-1970). Born, Cambuslang; studied at Glasgow School of Art under Frä Newberry (*q.v.*); in London from 1919 where he associated with vorticists such as Wyndham Lewis and Bomberg.

McCULLOCH, HORATIO (1805-1867). Born, Glasgow; apprenticed to house-painter; removed to Edinburgh, 1838; painted landscapes of Scottish scenery. A.R.S.A., 1834; R.S.A., 1838. Died, Edinburgh. **£30-480.**

MACDONALD, MISS FRANCES (1874-1921). Associated with the Glasgow School and wife of Herbert MacNair; portraits and figure subjects.

McDONALD, JOHN BLAKE (1829-1901). Born, Boharm; pupil of Robert Scott Lauder; painted incidents from the Jacobite Rebellion and later moved on to landscapes. A.R.S.A., 1862; R.S.A., 1877. Died, Edinburgh. **£35-155.**

MACDONALD, MARGARET (1865-1933). Sister of Frances Macdonald (*q.v.*); studied G.S.A. and introduced by Fra Newberry (*q.v.*) to Charles Rennie Mackintosh (*q.v.*), whom she married in 1900; decorative work incorporated in many of Mackintosh's designs.

McDOUGALL, LILY M. M. (1875-1958). Born, Glasgow; lived and worked in Edinburgh; still-life in oil and watercolour; exhibited R.S.A., R.S.W., G.I. **£10.**

MACDOUGALL, NORMAN M. (*fl.* 1870-1920). Lived Glasgow; exhibited R.A., R.B.A., R.I. and Glasgow Institute; figure paintings. **£70-140.**

McEWAN, TOM (1846-1914). Glasgow artist; genre paintings. **£220-420.**

McGEEHAN, J. M. (19th century). Painter in oils of genre subjects and scenes of domestic life. **£400-£850.**

MacGEORGE, WILLIAM STEWART (1861-1931). Born, Castle Douglas; in 1880 entered Royal Institution, Edinburgh, as student; later went to Antwerp with E. A. Hornel; associated with Glasgow School; painted landscapes with figures. A.R.S.A., 1898; R.S.A., 1910. Died, Gifford. **£150-600.**

McGHIE, JOHN (born 1867). Studied G.S.A., R.A. Schools and Paris (Academie Julien); exhibited R.A., R.S.A. and Paris Salon; lived in Glasgow; painter and etcher of coastal scenes, figures and portraits. **£100, 180 (w).**

McGILL, DUNCAN T. G. (born 1896). Studied Edinburgh College of Art and exhibited R.A., R.S.A., R.S.W., S.S.A., G.I.; landscapes in oil and watercolour.

McGLASHAN, ARCHIBALD A. (born 1888). Born Paisley; studied G.S.A. under Newbery (*q.v.*); exhibited R.S.A., R.I., G.I.; travelled on the Continent and lived in Glasgow; noted for portraits in oil. A.R.S.A., 1935; R.S.A., 1939. **£40-65.**

MacGOUN, HANNAH PRESTON (1864-1913). Studied at Edinburgh School of Art and R.S.A. Life School; painted genre subjects and children, chiefly watercolour; illustrated works of Dr John Brown. R.S.W., 1903.

McGREGOR, ROBERT (1847-1922). Born, Yorkshire; worked with his father at damask designing, Dunfermline; studied in R.S.A. Schools; painted figure subjects with village or landscape settings. A.R.S.A., 1882; R.S.A., 1889. Died, Portobello, nr. Edinburgh. **£70-360.**

MacGREGOR, SARA (*fl.* 1900-1920). Exhibited R.S.A.; portraits and figure paintings. **£100-900.**

MACGREGOR, WILLIAM YORK (1855-1923). Born, Finnart, Loch Goil; studied under James Docharty; later at Slade School, London; "father" of the Glasgow School; painted landscapes. A.R.S.A., 1898; R.S.A., 1921. Died at Bridge of Allan, nr. Stirling. **£11-28 (w).**

McIAN, ROBERT RANALD (1803-1856). Lived in Edinburgh and London; artist and printmaker specialising in Highland scenes, people and events; exhibited R.S.A., 1840-1863; A.R.S.A., 1852. **£100 (w).**

McINNES, ALEXANDER (*fl. c.* 1845). Inverness artist; exhibited R.S.A., 1842-1844; local scenes.

MACKAY, CHARLES (1868-?). Born, Glasgow; studied G.S.A. and Paris (Academie Delecluse); exhibited R.S.A., G.I.; landscapes in watercolour.

McKAY, T. H. (*c.* (1870-1920). Painter in oil of Highland landscapes. **£28-120.**

McKAY, WILLIAM DARLING (1844-1924). Born, Haddington; studied at Edinburgh School of Art and

R.S.A. life classes; painted landscapes; author of *Scottish School of Painting*, etc. A.R.S.A., 1877; R.S.A., 1883. Died, Edinburgh. **£70-320, 800 (1975).**

MACKELLAR, DUNCAN (1849-1908). Born, Glasgow; studied Glasgow and London; exhibited R.I., R.A. and Grosvenor Gallery from 1883; genre paintings; R.S.W. Died, Glasgow. **£220-270.**

McKECHNIE, ALEXANDER BALFOUR (1860-1930). Born, Paisley; studied G.S.A.; painted landscapes and eastern subjects in oil and watercolour. R.S.W. Died, Milliken Park.

MACKENZIE, JAMES HAMILTON (1875-1926). Born, Glasgow; studied at Glasgow School of Art and in Italy; painted landscapes abroad and among Western Isles of Scotland; many fine pastels. R.S.W., 1910; A.R.S.A., 1923; A.R.E. **£12 (p), 30-48.**

MACKENZIE, ALEXANDER (1850-1890). Born, Aberdeen; genre painting.

MACKENZIE, SAMUEL (1785-1847). Lived and worked in Edinburgh; exhibited R.S.A. from 1827; portraits; R.S.A., 1829.

MACKIE, CHARLES H. (1862-1920). Born, Aldershot, son of an army officer; student at R.S.A. Schools; worked at applied art and mural decoration; later, portraiture and landscape. A.R.S.A., 1902; R.S.A., 1917. Died, Edinburgh. **£62-125.**

MACKINNON, ESTHER BLAIKIE (1885-1935). Born, Aberdeen.

MACKINTOSH, CHARLES RENNIE (1868-1928). Born, Glasgow; apprenticed as architect, 1887; studied at Glasgow School of Art and in France and Italy; removed to London and practised as architect and painter in watercolour. Died, London. **£500 (w).**

McLACHLAN, JOHN (*fl.* 1880-1890). Exhibited R.S.A., 1881-1892.

McLACHLAN, THOMAS HOPE (1845-1897). Gave up law for art; largely self-taught with a period in Paris; rural and pastoral scenes, landscapes.

MACLAREN, JOHN STEWART (1860-1930?). Born, Edinburgh; studied R.S.A. Schools and Paris; exhibited R.A., G.I.; R.S.A.; oils and watercolours of figures, landscapes and architectural subjects.

McLAURIN, DUNCAN (1849-1921). Born, Glasgow; studied Glasgow School of Design and Heatherley's; lived in Helensburgh; landscapes and cattle; R.S.W.

MACLEAY, KENNETH (1802-1878). Foundation Associate of the Scottish Academy; miniature painter who devoted himself to portraiture; much in demand for commissions; best work in watercolour. A.R.S.A., 1826; R.S.A., 1829. Died, Edinburgh. **£30-42 (w).**

MacLEAY, McNEIL (1802-1878). Born, Oban; painter of grand, dramatic Highland landscapes, especially west

coast of Scotland; A.R.S.A., 1836-1848. Died, Oban.
£110-150, 800 (1975).

McLELLAN, ALEXANDER MATHESON (1872-1957).
Born, Greenock; studied R.A. Schools and Paris; worked
Paris, London, Manchester, New York and Glasgow;
exhibited R.A., R.S.A., R.O.I., R.B.A., R.S.W., Paris
Salon; portraits and figures in oil and watercolour;
R.B.A.; R.S.W.

MACMASTER, JAMES (1856-1913). Exhibited
Edinburgh and London; lived Glasgow; Scottish and
Dutch landscape and coastal scenes in oil and water-
colour; R.S.W. **£80, 54 (w).**

MacMORLAND, PATRICK (1741-c. 1809). Born,
Scotland; painted miniatures, Manchester and Liverpool;
exhibited 1774-82 at R.A. and Scottish Academy.

MACNEE, SIR DANIEL (1806-1882). Born, Fintry;
resided in Glasgow; apprenticed, 1820, to John Knox,
landscape painter (*q.v.*); devoted himself to portraiture.
R.S.A., 1829; P.R.S.A., 1876; knighted, 1876. Died,
Edinburgh. **£180, 150 (pair).**

MACNEE, ROBERT RUSSELL (1880-1952). Born,
Milngavie; painter of fine rural scenes and incidents,
often connected with farming. **£38-350.**

MacNICOL, BESSIE (1869-1904). Born, Glasgow;
studied at Glasgow School of Art and Paris; influenced
by the Glasgow School; competent illustrator; worked in
oil and watercolour; married Alexander Frew. Died,
Glasgow. **£190.**

MACNIVEN, JOHN (*fl.* 1880-1890). Born and worked in Glasgow; local scenes. Exhibited R.S.A., 1884-1892; R.S.W. **£30.**

McTAGGART, WILLIAM (1835-1910). Born, Aros, nr. Campbeltown, Argyllshire; studied at Trustees' Academy, Edinburgh, with Chalmers, Pettie, Orchardson, etc.; chiefly painted landscape, and children in sea-shore or rural setting, with special study of light and movement. A.R.S.A., 1859; R.S.A., 1870. Died, Dean Mark, Broomieknowe, Midlothian. **£380-1,000, 150-300 (w).**

MACWHIRTER, JOHN (1839-1911). Born, Slateford, nr. Edinburgh; studied at Trustees' Academy, Edinburgh, with Chalmers, Orchardson, Pettie, etc.; settled in London; painted landscapes, principally in Scottish Highlands. A.R.S.A., 1869; A.R.A., 1879; R.A., 1893. Died, London. **£130-340, 50-100 (w).**

MANN, ALEXANDER (1853-1908). Born, Glasgow; pupil of Carolus Duran; exhibited extensively; travelled and painted in Italy, France and Morocco; genre paintings and Scottish landscape with highly developed sense of atmosphere and subdued colours. R.A. Died, London. **£340 (1975).**

MANN, HARRINGTON (1864-1937). Born, Glasgow; studied at Slade School, London, and in Paris and Rome; from 1890-1900 painted figure subjects and portraits in Glasgow; settling in London, became known for portraits of children; worked much in U.S.A. Member of New English Art Club and International Society.

MANSON, GEORGE (1850-1876). Born, Edinburgh; began his career as a wood engraver before turning to watercolour; figure painting and architectural subjects. Died, Lympstone.

MARTIN, DAVID (1736-1798). Born, Anstruther; pupil of Allan Ramsay in London; practised as portrait painter in London; Limner to the Prince of Wales; moved to Edinburgh; also engraver in mezzotint and line. Died, Edinburgh.

MARTIN, DAVID (fl. 1890-1920). Author and painter; friend of Frä Newberry (q.v.); wrote *The Glasgow School of Painting* (1897); favourite medium, watercolour, usually coast or harbour scenes. **£26-90 (w).**

MELVILLE, ARTHUR (1830-1923). Born, Loanhead of Guthrie, Forfar; self-taught; in 1877 studied at Paris; visited Egypt, India, Persia, 1881-82; spent some years in Scotland, associated with Glasgow School; developed personal method of watercolour; worked much in Spain and Morocco. A.R.S.A., 1886; A.R.W.S., 1889; R.W.S., 1900. **£175-1,000 (w).**

MICHIE, JAMES COUTTS (1861-1919). Born, Aboyne; fine winter landscapes; views in north-east Scotland. A.R.S.A., 1893. Died, Haslemere. **£100 (1975).**

MILLAR, WILLIAM (dates uncertain). Portrait painter, mid-18th Century. Works noted, c. 1750-70.

MILLER, JAMES (born, 1893). Born, Glasgow; studied G.S.A. under Frä Newberry (q.v.); travelled then to Paris and has subsequently travelled extensively in Europe; favourite subjects are architectural in nature and are generally painted in watercolour. A.R.S.A., 1943; R.S.A., 1964; R.S.W.

MILNE, JOHN MACLAUGHLAN (1886-1957). Born, Edinburgh; studied Edinburgh College of Art and Paris; visited France and painted subjects there; landscapes and still life in oil and watercolour; A.R.S.A., 1933; R.S.A. 1937. Died, Isle of Arran. **£130-300.**

MILNE, JOSEPH (1861-1911). Lived in Edinburgh; painted the towns and fishing villages on the east coast of Scotland; atmospheric pictures with good use of colour. Died, Edinburgh. **£38-130.**

MITCHELL, JOHN (1838-1926). Born, Aberdeen; painted views and subjects in north-east Scotland.

MITCHELL, JOHN CAMPBELL (1862-1922). Born, Campbeltown; worked in lawyer's office; in 1884 entered Edinburgh School of Art; worked in R.S.A. Life Class and at Paris; painted landscape and seascape. A.R.S.A., 1904; R.S.A., 1918. Died, Edinburgh. **£140.**

MITCHELL, MADGE YOUNG (1892-1973). Born, Uddingston; lived in Aberdeen and taught at Grays School of Art.

MOODIE, DONALD (1892-1963). Born, Edinburgh; taught Edinburgh College of Art; wide range of subjects. A.R.S.A., 1943; R.S.A., 1952; President S.S.A., 1937-1942.

MORE, JACOB (1740-1793). Born, Edinburgh; worked in Italy, painted landscapes, known as "More of Rome". Died, Rome.

MORTON, THOMAS CORSAN (1859-1928). Born, Glasgow; studied at Glasgow School of Art and Slade School, London, later in Paris; associated with founders of Glasgow School; Keeper of N.G. of Scotland; Curator of Art Gallery, Kirkcaldy. Died, Kirkcaldy. **£58.**

MOSMAN, WILLIAM (*c.* 1700-1771). Active from about 1730; teacher of drawing at King's and Marischal Colleges, Aberdeen; painted portraits and landscapes. Died, Middlefield, nr. Aberdeen.

MOUNCEY, WILLIAM (1852-1901). Born, Kirkcudbright; married sister of E. A. Hornel (*q.v.*); retired from business as house decorator, *c.* 1886; painted landscapes. Died, Kirkcudbright. **£65-240.**

MUIRHEAD, DAVID (1867-1930). Born, Edinburgh; started as architect; studied painting at R.S.A. Schools, and at Westminster, under Professor Fred. Brown; painted portraits and landscapes in oil and watercolour. A.R.W.S.; A.R.A., 1928. Died, London.

MUIRHEAD, JOHN (1863-1927). Born, Edinburgh; studied at the Board of Manufacturers' School; exhibited R.S.A., R.A., R.I., N.E.A.C.; worked in Europe; R.S.W., 1893; R.B.A., 1902.

MONRO, ALEXANDER BINNING (1805-1891). Admitted W.S. but did not practise; exhibited R.S.A; R.S.A., 1826.

MONRO, CHARLES CARMICHAEL BINNING (1851-?). Fourth son of Alex. Binning Monro (*q.v.*); painter of seascapes; exhibited London, 1874-90.

MUNRO, DANIEL (*fl.* 1850-1870). Exhibited R.S.A., 1846-1872; genre paintings. **£220 (1975).**

MUNRO, HUGH (1872-1939). Born, Glasgow; entered business but concentrated on art from 1905; landscapes and Highland subjects; exhibited R.S.A. Died, Glasgow. **£45-110.**

MUNRO or MONRO, ROBERT (died 1829). Portrait painter based in Montrose; died Montrose, Spetember 6, 1829.

MOORE, ELEANOR A. (1885-1955). Born, Glenwherry, Northern Ireland; studied G.S.A.; painted portraits in oil and, as (Mrs) E. A. Robertson, water-colour studies of Chinese people and landscapes. Died, Edinburgh.

MUIR, ANNE DAVIDSON (1875-1951). Born, Hawick; studied Edinburgh College of Art; 1923 awarded Lauder Prize at Glasgow Lady Artists' Exhibition; specialised in paintings of flowers. Died, Edinburgh.

MURRAY, SIR DAVID (1849-1934). Born, Glasgow; worked in mercantile firm; studied at Glasgow School of Art; removed to London, 1883; painted landscapes in oil and watercolour. A.R.S.A., 1881; H.R.S.A., 1919; A.R.W.S., 1886; P.R.I., 1917; A.R.A., 1891; R.A., 1905; knighted, 1918. Died, London. **£80-440, 55 (w).**

SAMUEL BOUGH (1822-1878)
London from Shooters Hill
Sold by Sotheby's in Scotland
£14,000

JOSEPH FARQUHARSON (1847-1935)
Winter, Finzean
Sold by Sotheby's in Scotland
£3,600

MURRAY, THOMAS (1666-1724). Born, Scotland; went to London at early age and studied under Riley; had great success in portraiture.

MURRAY, WILLIAM GRANT (1877-1950). Born, Portsoy; watercolours of Banffshire coast.

MYLES, W. S. Forfar artist, exhibited R.S.A. from 1886. **£26-55.**

NASMYTH, ALEXANDER (1758-1840). Born, Edinburgh; studied under A. Runciman and Allan Ramsay, later in Italy; painted landscapes and portraits, including Robert Burns. Died, Edinburgh. **£300-4,000 for view of Perth.**

NASMYTH, ANNE. Daughter of Alexander Nasmyth; painted landscape in the style of her father and assisted him in the teaching of art in Edinburgh. **£2,000.**

NASMYTH, CHARLOTTE. Youngest daughter of Alexander Nasmyth; exhibited R.S.A. 1831-1862; assisted her father in the teaching of art in Edinburgh. **£520.**

NASMYTH, JAMES (died 1866). Youngest son of Alexander Nasmyth.

NASMYTH, MARGARET. Daughter of Alexander Nasmyth; painted in the style of her father and assisted him in his teaching. **£2,000.**

NASMYTH, PATRICK (1787-1831). Born, Edinburgh; eldest son and pupil of Alex. Nasmyth; studied under

Alex. Runciman and Allan Ramsay, and afterwards in Italy; painted landscapes and portraits, including that of Robert Burns. Died, Lambeth. **£400-750.**

NEWBERRY, FRANCIS HENRY (1855-1946). Born, Membury; exhibited R.A. from 1890; director of G.S.A. from 1885 and commissioned Charles Rennie Mackintosh (*q.v.*) to design the new school, 1897; under his guidance G.S.A. became one of the most successful art schools in Europe; all subjects in oil and watercolour. Died, Corfe.

NICHOLSON, P. W. (1856-1885). Trained as a lawyer but went to Ruskin Drawing School, Oxford, 1878, and was influenced by Turner; travelled to Paris, 1881, and did much interesting work in watercolour before a premature death through drowning; pastoral themes.

NICHOLSON, WILLIAM (1781-1844). Born, Newcastle upon Tyne; foundation member of the Scottish Academy; Academy secretary 1826-1830; painter and etcher. R.S.A., 1826. Died, Edinburgh.

NICOL, ERSKINE (1825-1904). Born, Leith; studied at Trustees' Academy; removed to Dublin, and painted humorous side of Irish life; later, worked in Edinburgh and in England. A.R.S.A., 1855; R.S.A., 1859; A.R.A., 1866. Died, Feltham, Middlesex. **£50-1,050.**

NICOL, GEORGE SMITH (*fl.* 1850-1880). Exhibited R.S.A., 1851-1879.

NISBET, ROBERT BUCHAN (1857-1942). Born, Edinburgh; brother of Pollok Nisbet (*q.v.*); studied Edinburgh at R.S.A. Life School and Paris under

Bouguereau; specialised in Scottish landscapes in watercolour; popular abroad. A.R.S.A., 1893; R.S.A., 1902; R.S.W.; R.I.; R.B.A. Died, Crieff. **£100 (w).**

NISBET, POLLOK SINCLAIR (1848-1922). Born, Edinburgh; travelled abroad in Italy, Spain and North Africa; some excellent paintings of market places and mosques in Morocco and Spain; also painted Highland landscapes. A.R.S.A., 1892; R.S.W. Died, Edinburgh. **£50, 400 (1975).**

NOBLE, JAMES CAMPBELL (1846-1913). Born, Edinburgh; studied at School of Art and R.S.A. Schools; began as painter of figure subjects; afterwards exclusively landscapes. A.R.S.A., 1879; R.S.A., 1892. Died, Ledaig, Argyllshire. **£40-180.**

NOBLE, ROBERT (1857-1917). Born, Edinburgh; studied at R.S.A. Life School and at Paris; painted cottage interiors, French street scenes, and afterwards his native landscape. A.R.S.A., 1892; R.S.A., 1903. Died, East Linton. **£150-400.**

NORIE, JAMES (1684-1757). Born, Knockando; classical landscapes.

OPPENHEIMER, CHARLES (1875-1961). Born, Manchester; studied under Walter Crane at Manchester School of Art and later in Italy; lived and painted for 52 years in Kirkcudbright; many very fine landscapes of Galloway. A.R.S.A., 1927; R.S.A., 1934; R.S.W. Died, Kirkcudbright. **£50 (w).**

ORCHARDSON, Sir WILLIAM QUILLER (1832-1910). Born, Edinburgh; studied at Trustees' Academy under Scott Lauder, with Pettie, P. Graham, etc.; in 1862 settled in London; painted portraits, pictures of social incident and manners, and episodes from Napoleonic period. A.R.A., 1868; R.A., 1877; H.R.S.A., 1871; knighted, 1907. **£180 (1975).**

ORR, MONRO SCOTT (born 1874). Born, Irvine; studied G.S.A.; exhibited R.S.A., R.S.W. and Glasgow Institute; book illustrator, painter and etcher.

ORR, STEWART (1872-1945). Born, Glasgow; studied G.S.A.; exhibited R.S.A., R.S.W., Glasgow Institute; R.S.W., 1925; lived Corrie, Isle of Arran. **£10 (w).**

OSWALD, JOHN HARVEY (*fl.* 1870-1899). Lived, Edinburgh; painted landscapes and seascapes; exhibited R.S.A.; R.S.W.; R.A.; R.H.A.

PARK, JAMES STUART (1862-1933). Born, Kidderminster, of Ayrshire parents; studied at Glasgow School of Art, and in Paris; painted figure subjects and portraits, but best known as flower painter; associated with Glasgow School. Died, Kilmarnock. **£50-380.**

PATERSON, EMILY MURRAY (1855-1934). Born, Edinburgh; studied at Edinburgh Art School, and in Paris; painted watercolours mostly in Holland, Switzerland, Venice; in later life resided in London. Member of R.S.W. Died, London. **£40, 28 (w).**

PATERSON, JAMES (1854-1932). Born, Glasgow; studied at Glasgow School of Art, and in Paris; worked on Continent, and finally settled at Moniaive, Dumfriesshire; painted landscapes in oil and watercolour. A.R.S.A., 1896; R.S.A., 1910; R.S.W., 1885; P.R.S.W., 1916; R.W.S., 1898. Died, Edinburgh. **£60, 20-140 (w).**

PATON, DAVID (*fl.* 1650-1700). Painted portraits and miniatures in plumbago and sepia.

PATON, Sir JOSEPH NOEL (1821-1901). Born, Dunfermline; removed to London, 1843; studied in R.A. Schools; gained premium for Westminster Hall fresco, 1844; painted religious and romantic subjects. A.R.S.A., 1846; R.S.A., 1850; Queen's Limner for Scotland, 1866; knighted, 1867. Died, Edinburgh. **£60 (w), 420.**

PATON, WALLER HUGH (1828-1895). Born, Dunfermline; brother of Sir Joseph Noel Paton (*q.v.*); trained R.S.A. Schools; highly individual style of watercolour; Scottish Highland landscapes and views. A.R.S.A., 1858; R.S.A., 1865; R.S.W. Died, Edinburgh. **£350, 950 (1975), 50-320 (w).**

PEPLOE, SAMUEL JOHN (1871-1935). Born, Edinburgh; entered Edinburgh University; studied Law; in 1902 worked in R.S.A. Life School, and later in Paris; in Paris for some years after 1910, and frequently painted in France; settled in Edinburgh, and worked at landscape, figure and particularly still life. A.R.S.A., 1918; R.S.A., 1927. **£200-3,000, 160 (w).**

PERIGAL, ARTHUR (1816-1884). Born, London; landscapes in Scotland in oil and watercolour. A.R.S.A., 1841; R.S.A., 1868; R.S.W. Died, Edinburgh. **£280-420, 30-48 (w).**

PERMAN, LOUISE (died 1921). Born, near Glasgow; studied at Glasgow School of Art; married James Torrance, 1912; painted flower pieces. Died, Helensburgh. **£48.**

PETTIE, JOHN (1839-1893). Born, Edinburgh; studied at Trustees' Academy under Scott Lauder, with Orchardson, Hugh Cameron, etc.; in 1862 removed to London; painted romantic and historical incidents, themes from Scott and Shakespeare, portraits. A.R.A., 1866; R.A., 1873; H.R.S.A., 1871. Lived in London from 1862-93. Died, Hastings. **£135-340.**

PHILLIP, JOHN 1817-1867), popularly known as "Spanish Phillip". Born, Aberdeen; in 1837 entered R.A. Schools, London; at Aberdeen, 1840 to 1846, painting portraits; settled in London and painted Scottish domestic life; visited Spain in 1851 and produced a series of pictures of Spanish life. A.R.A., 1857; R.A., 1859. Died, London. **£380.**

PIRIE, Sir GEORGE (1866-1946). Born, Campbeltown; studied Glasgow University and Paris under Boulanger and Lefevre; travelled to America in the 1890s; animals his favourite subject matter. A.R.S.A., 1913; R.S.A., 1923; S.S.A., P.R.S.A.; H.R.A.; H.R.S.W. Died, Torrance. **£120 (1975).**

POWELL, Sir FRANCIS (1833-1914). Born, Manchester; studied Manchester and moved to Scotland; President Scottish Society of Painters in Watercolour, 1878; A.R.W.S., 1867; R.W.S., 1876; knighted, 1893; Landscape and marine subjects in watercolour. Died, Dunoon.

PRINGLE, JOHN QUINTON (1864-1925). Born, Glasgow; optician by profession; studied at Glasgow School of Art; painted miniatures and street scenes. Died, Glasgow. **£145 (w).**

PRYDE, JAMES F. (1866-1941). Born, Edinburgh; studied R.S.A. Schools, 1886, and Academie Julien, Paris, under Bouguereau; settled London, 1890, and produced posters with his brother-in-law, William Nicholson, under name "J. and W. Beggarstaff"; exhibited Baillie Gallery, Goupil Gallery, Leicester Galleries; responsible for theatre decor, architectural fantasies and interiors.

RAEBURN, AGNES (1872-1955). Born, Glasgow; studied G.S.A. 1890-94; exhibited widely in Scotland, Paris, U.S. and Canada; landscapes and flower studies in watercolour; Lauder Prize in 1927; R.S.W., 1901. Died, Edinburgh.

RAEBURN, ETHEL (1867-1953). Born, Edinburgh; exhibited R.S.A., 1892, 1905-1945; travelled and painted in France and Italy.

RAEBURN, Sir HENRY (1756-1823). Born, Stockbridge, Edinburgh; educated at Heriot's Hospital;

apprenticed at age 15 to Gilliland, goldsmith, and painted miniatures; visited London, and was encouraged by Sir J. Reynolds; spent two years in Italy; in 1787 settled in Edinburgh as portrait painter. President, Society of Scottish Painters (R.S.A.), 1812; A.R.A., 1812; R.A., 1815; knighted by George IV, 1822; King's Limner for Scotland, 1823. Died, Edinburgh.

RAMSAY, ALLAN (1713-1784). Born, Edinburgh; eldest son of Allan Ramsay, poet; pupil in London of Hans Huyssing, studied historical painting in Italy, 1736-1738; settled in London and devoted himself to portraiture; friend of Dr Johnson, Horace Walpole, Voltaire and Rousseau; appointed principal portrait painter to George III, 1761; for many years had studio in Edinburgh. Died, Dover.

RATTRAY, ALEXANDER WELLWOOD (1849-1902). Born, St Andrews; lived and worked in Glasgow; exhibited R.S.A., 1876-1902; landscapes and seascapes of Scotland. A.R.S.A., 1896; R.S.W. Died, Glasgow. **£42-160.**

READ, CATHERINE (died 1778). Daughter of Forfarshire gentleman of Jacobite leanings; studied in Paris and Italy; painted notabilities in oil and crayon; in 1775 went to India. Died on homeward voyage.

REDPATH, ANNE (1895-1965). Born, Galashiels; studied at Edinburgh College of Art, 1913-1919; visited Paris and Florence, living in Paris until 1934; returned to Scotland and became President, S.W.A., 1944-1947; R.B.A., 1946; A.R.S.A., 1947; R.S.A., 1952; R.O.I., 1948; O.B.E.,

1955; R.W.A., 1957; A.R.A., 1960; A.R.W.S., 1962.
£260-950, 260 (w).

REID, ALEX (1854-1928). Born, Glasgow; best known as the important and influential Glasgow art dealer; exhibited watercolours at the Glasgow Fine Art Institute in the 1870s; painted in Paris, influenced by Van Gogh. Died, Killearn.

REID, ARCHIBALD DAVID (1844-1908). Born, Aberdeen; studied R.S.A. Life Class and Paris; toured Holland, France and Spain; at his best in Highland landscapes. A.R.S.A., 1892.

REID, Sir GEORGE (1841-1913). Born, Aberdeen; Apprenticed to lithographer; studied in Edinburgh and Paris; painted portraits, landscapes, flower pieces; made pen-and-ink drawings. A.R.S.A., 1870; R.S.A., 1877; P.R.S.A. and knighted, 1891. After 1910 removed to Somersetshire, where he died. **£520.**

REID, GEORGE OGILVY (1851-1928). Born, Leith; painted, in watercolour and oil, subjects dealing with Jacobite and earlier periods. A.R.S.A., 1888; R.S.A., 1898. Died, Edinburgh. **£22-42.**

REID, JOHN ROBERTSON (1851-1926). Born, Edinburgh; studied at R.S.A. Schools; in 1881 went to Cornwall, where he worked for 20 years; painted landscapes and scenes of fishing life. Died, London. **£60-240.**

REID, ROBERT PAYTON (born 1859). Lived and worked in Edinburgh, 1880-1915; classical and mythological themes. A.R.S.A., 1896. **£165-300.**

RENISON, WILLIAM (*fl.* 1920s). Born, Glasgow; exhibited R.A., Glasgow Institute and Paris Salon; landscapes and architecture.

RIDDEL, JAMES (1857-1928). Born, Glasgow; studied G.S.A. and later in Edinburgh; painted landscapes and was influenced by his friend, J. Lawton Wingate (*q.v.*). A.R.S.A., 1919; R.S.W. Died, Balerno. **£17.**

ROBERTS, DAVID (1796-1864). Born, Stockbridge, Edinburgh; worked as house painter; then as scene painter in Carlisle and Edinburgh; in 1822, at Drury Lane and Covent Garden, London; in 1824 visited Normandy and later travelled over Europe, Syria, Egypt; painted landscapes and architecture in oil and water-colour. A.R.A., 1838; R.A., 1841; H.R.S.A., 1829. Died, London.

ROBERTSON, ALEXANDER (1772-1841). Born, Aberdeen; brother of Andrew Robertson and pupil of Shelley in London; like his brother, Archibald, he went to America; miniature painter. Died, New York.

ROBERTSON, ANDREW (1777-1845). Born, Aberdeen; had lessons in Edinburgh from Raeburn, and practised as teacher in Aberdeen; in 1797 entered R.A. Schools and settled in London; had large practice as painter of portraits in miniature. Died, London.

ROBERTSON, ERIC (1887-1941). Born, Dumfries; studied Edinburgh College of Art; exhibited regularly at S.S.A. and R.S.A.; all media; married Cecile Walton (*q.v.*), daughter of E. A. Walton (*q.v.*); left Edinburgh 1924. Died, Cheshire. **£92.**

ROBERTSON, TOM (1850-1947). Born, Glasgow; landscapes.

ROCHE, ALEXANDER IGNATIUS (1861-1921). Born, Glasgow; studied in Glasgow and Paris; in 1883 returned Glasgow and became associated with Glasgow School; settled Edinburgh, 1896; painted figure subjects, landscapes, portraits, wall decoration; worked from 1908 with left hand, owing to paralysis of right. A.R.S.A., 1893; R.S.A., 1900. **£50-300, 500 (1975).**

ROSS, JOSEPH THORBURN (1849-1903). Lived and worked in Edinburgh; exhibited R.S.A., 1872-1904; landscapes, seascapes, birds and children. A.R.S.A., 1896. Died, Edinburgh.

ROSS, Sir WILLIAM CHARLES (1794-1860). Born, London; studied in R.A. Schools; painted classical subjects, then miniatures; for a time assistant to Andrew Robertson; painted over 2,200 miniatures. A.R.A., 1838; R.A., 1839; knighted, 1839.

RUNCIMAN, ALEXANDER (1736-1785). Born, Edinburgh; apprenticed to John Norie, decorator; studied at Foulis' Academy, Glasgow, and in Rome; there in close touch with Fuseli; in 1771 appointed Master of Trustees' Academy, Edinburgh; decorated hall of

Penicuik House with subjects from Ossian (destroyed by fire, 1899). Died, Edinburgh.

RUNCIMAN, JOHN (1744-1769). Born, Edinburgh; younger brother of Alex. Runciman; accompanied his brother to Rome; painted with much imaginative feeling. Died, Naples.

RUSSELL, CHARLES (1852-1910). Born Dumbarton; portrait painter in watercolour and oil; moved from Scotland to Dublin in 1874.

SANDERS, GEORGE (1774-1846). Born, Kinghorn, Fife; apprenticed to coachpainter; painted miniatures and taught drawing; in 1807 moved to London and became popular miniaturist; also painted oil portraits. Died, London.

SCOTT, DAVID (1806-1949). Born, Edinburgh; apprenticed to his father as line engraver; studied at Trustees' Academy; visited Italy, 1832-34; painted imaginative and poetical works and historical subjects. A.R.S.A., 1829; R.S.A., 1834. Died, Edinburgh.

SCOTT, THOMAS (1854-1927). Born, Selkirk; studied at Edinburgh School and R.S.A. Life Class; painted landscapes of the Border country. A.R.S.A., 1888; R.S.A., 1902. Died, Selkirk. **£25-160 (w).**

SCOTT, WILLIAM BELL (1811-1890). Born, Edinburgh; studied as engraver under his father; as painter, at Trustees' Academy, and under his brother,

David Scott; moved to London and painted romantic and historical subjects; in 1843 became Master of Newcastle School of Design; intimate friend of Rossetti and his circle; wrote various books on art. H.R.S.A., 1887.

SCOUGALL, DAVID (early 17th century). Portrait painter.

SCOUGALL, JOHN, Senr. (mid-17th century). Portrait painter.

SCOUGALL, JOHN, Junr. (1645?-1730). Had house and studio in Advocate's Close, Edinburgh; painted portraits dated from 1670; retired about 1715.

SELLAR, CHARLES A. (*fl.* 1880-1930). Painter of portraits, people and coast scenes; exhibited R.A., R.S.W. and G.I.; R.S.W.; lived, Perth. **£68.**

SETON, JOHN THOMAS (worked *c.* 1760-1780). Son of Christopher Seton, gem engraver; studied under Hayman and exhibited at R.A.; settled in Scotland and painted many portraits. Living in 1806.

SHANKS, WILLIAM SOMERVILLE (1864-1951). Born, Gourock; attended evening classes at G.S.A. under Frä Newberry and later studied in Paris under Laurens and Constant; exhibited at Paris Salon; lived in Glasgow and painted all types of subject. A.R.S.A., 1923; R.S.A., 1933. **£65.**

SHERIFF, JOHN (1816-1844). Lived and worked in Edinburgh; exhibited R.S.A. from 1830; animals and portraits. A.R.S.A., 1839.

SHERRIFFS, A. JOHN (*fl.* 1890-1894). Active in Aberdeen during the period painting local subjects.

SHIELS, WILLIAM (1785-1857). Foundation Academician; lived in Edinburgh and Kelso; exhibited R.S.A. from 1827; animals, birds and people. R.S.A., 1826.

SHIRREFF, CHARLES (*c.* 1750-*c.* 1831). Deaf and dumb artist; first practised in Edinburgh and later came to London; exhibited, Society of Artists, 1770-1772, in crayons; at Bath, 1794; visited India, 1796-1797; exhibited, 1770-1831 at R.A. etc.

SIMPSON, WILLIAM (1823-1899). Born, Glasgow; studied as architect; went to London 1851 and became war correspondent in Crimea, 1854; illustrated travels, etc. R.I. Died, London. **£22.**

SIMSON, GEORGE (1791-1862). Born, Edinburgh; lived and worked in Edinburgh; exhibited R.S.A., 1830-1863; landscapes and seascapes. A.R.S.A., 1826; R.S.A., 1829. Died, Edinburgh.

SIMSON, WILLIAM (1800-1847). Born, Dundee; studied at Trustees' Academy, Edinburgh; visited Italy, 1835; returned from Continent, 1838, and settled in London; painted landscapes, coast scenes and, later, figure subjects. R.S.A., 1829. Died, London.

SINCLAIR, ALEXANDER GARDEN (1859-1930). Born, Kenmore, Perthshire; studied at Aberdeen

University and then art at Trustee's Academy and R.S.A. Life School; painted Scottish landscape and portraits in oil; worked also in watercolour and pastel. A.R.S.A. **£20 (w).**

SIVELL, ROBERT (1888-1958). Born, Paisley; studied G.S.A. where he associated with Cowie and McGlashan (*q.v.*); Head of Gray's School of Art. A.R.S.A., 1936; R.S.A., 1943.

SKENE, JAMES, of Rubislaw (1775-1864). Born, Aberdeen; friend of Sir Walter Scott; amateur artist, also etcher and lithographer. Died, Oxford.

SMART, JOHN (1838-1899). Born, Leith; pupil of Horatio McCulloch (*q.v.*); exhibited widely; applied himself almost exclusively to painting landscapes of the Highlands; finest work, 1870-1890. A.R.S.A., 1871; R.S.A., 1877; R.S.W. Died, Leith. **£22-60, 65 (w).**

SMITH, CAMPBELL LINDSAY (1879-1915). Born, Forfarshire; portraits, animals and birds.

SMITH, COLVIN (1795-1875). Born, Brechin; studied at R.A. Schools, London; copied Old Masters in Italy; returned 1827 and settled as portrait painter in Edinburgh.

SMITH, GEORGE (1870-1934). Born, Mid Calder; studied at School of Bd. of Manufacturers, Edinburgh, and at Antwerp; on return worked in R.S.A. Life School; painted landscape. A.R.S.A., 1908; R.S.A., 1921; Died, Edinburgh. **£30-170.**

SOMERVILLE, ANDREW (1808-1834). Lived and worked in Edinburgh; exhibited R.S.A. from 1830; people and portraits. A.R.S.A., 1831; R.S.A., 1832.

SPENCE SMITH, JOHN G. (1880-1951). Born, Perth; studied Dundee College of Art and R.S.A. School; deaf and dumb from age of seven; painted landscapes and historic buildings. A.R.S.A., 1930; R.S.A., 1939. **£40.**

STANLEY, MONTAGUE (1809-1844). Lived and worked in Edinburgh; exhibited R.S.A., 1828-1845; Scottish landscapes. A.R.S.A., 1838; H.R.S.A., 1835-1838.

STANSMORE DEAN, RICHMOND LESLIE (1864-1944). Studied G.S.A. and Paris; 1902 married R. Macaulay Stevenson (*q.v.*); lived latterly at Kirkcudbright. Died, Castle Douglas.

STANTON, CLARK (1832-1894). Born, Birmingham; apprenticed in design and studied in Italy; returned to Britain 1885 and settled in Edinburgh; painting and sculpture of a decorative character, often drawing on classical themes. A.R.S.A., 1862; R.S.A., 1885; R.S.W. Died, Edinburgh. **£28 (w).**

STEEL, J. SYDNEY (1863-1932). Born, Perthshire; studied at the Slade School under Tonks; a keen naturalist, he was at his best painting deer and other animals; exhibited R.A. and one-man shows in London; co-illustrator, with John Quille Millais of *British Deer and Their Horns* (1897).

STEELL, DAVID GEORGE (1856-1930). Born, Edinburgh; son of Gourlay Steell (*q.v.*); animal painter. A.R.S.A., 1885. Died, Edinburgh. **£380.**

STEELL, GOURLAY (1819-1894). Born, Edinburgh; studied at Trustees' Academy under Scott Lauder (*q.v.*); appointed "Animal Painter for Scotland" by Queen Victoria and enjoyed considerable prestige; painter to the Highland and Agricultural Society. A.R.S.A., 1846; R.S.A., 1859.

STEVENS, JOHN (1793-1868). Scottish Academy Foundation Associate; exhibited R.S.A., 1827-1867; lived in London, Edinburgh and Rome. A.R.S.A., 1826; R.S.A., 1829.

STEVENSON, DAVID WATSON (1842-1904). Born, Ratho, Midlothian; pupil of W. Brodie, R.S.A.; studied in R.S.A. Schools and in Rome; sculptor of portrait busts and ideal subjects. A.R.S.A., 1877; R.S.A., 1886. Died, Edinburgh.

STEVENSON, ROBERT MACAULAY (1854-1952). Born, Glasgow; studied G.S.A. and associated closely with the Glasgow School; first exhibited in 1884 and thereafter frequently; one of the founders of the *Scottish Art Review*, 1888; France, 1910-1932; thereafter lived Kirkcudbright; oil and watercolour; penchant for moonlit scenes. R.S.W. Died, Milngavie. **£42-140.**

STEVENSON, WILLIAM GRANT (1849-1919). Born, Ratho; younger brother of D. W. Stevenson, R.S.A.; studied in Edinburgh School of Art and R.S.A. Life Class; as sculptor, executed large statues, portrait busts,

F

statuettes of animal life, etc. A.R.S.A., 1885; R.S.A., 1896. Died, Edinburgh. **£48.**

STEWART, JAMES (1791-1863). Born, Edinburgh; lived and worked in Edinburgh; exhibited R.S.A., 1830-1834; studied Trustees' Academy and became fine engraver; painter of portraits, landscape and genre; moved to London 1830 and emigrated to Cape Colony, 1833. R.S.A., 1829-1858; R.B.A. Died, Cape Colony.

STEWART, JAMES SCOTT. West of Scotland artist active in Glasgow area at the turn of the century; exhibited R.S.A.; R.S.W., 1880-1919. **£10 (p), 26 (w).**

STRACHAN, DOUGLAS (1875-1950). Born, Aberdeen; portraits, views at home and abroad, decorative and design work; stained glass; panels in public buildings. H.R.S.A.

STRANG, WILLIAM (1859-1921). Born, Dumbarton; studied at Slade School under Legros; painted allegorical subjects and portraits in oil, had wide range as etcher and engraver. A.R.A., 1906; R.A., 1921; President of International Society, 1918. Died, Bournemouth.

STURROCK, ALICK RIDDELL (1885-1953). Born, Edinburgh; apprenticed as a lithographic artist and later attended R.S.A. Life Class; travelling scholarship took him to Italy, Paris, Munich and Holland; known for his landscapes, especially of Solwayside. A.R.S.A., 1929; R.S.A., 1937. Died, Edinburgh. **£12-52.**

SUTHERLAND, DAVID M. (1883-1973). Born, Wick; forsook law for art; R.S.A. Life Class and on to Spain,

France and Holland; taught at Edinburgh College of Art, appointed Head of Gray's School of Art in 1933; fine oils of all types of subject but much influenced by West Coast of Scotland.   A.R.S.A., 1922; R.S.A., 1936.   Died, Plockton. **£60.**

SYME, JOHN (1795-1861).   Born, Edinburgh; studied in School of Bd. of Manufacturers and was assistant to Raeburn; painted portraits; one of original members of Scottish Academy. Died, Edinburgh.

SYME, PATRICK (1774-1845).   Born, Edinburgh; exhibited Society of Artists from 1808; known as a flower painter but also some portraits; 1810 published *Practical Directions for Learning Flower Drawing.* R.S.A., 1826.

TARBET, J. A. HENDERSON (*fl.* 1880-1912). Exhibited R.S.A.; painted Scottish landscapes. **£30-40 (w).**

TAYLOR, ERNEST ARCHIBALD (1874-1952).   Born, Greenock; exhibited R.S.A., R.S.W., G.I. and Paris Salon; married Jessie M. King (*q.v.*) and lived at Kirkcudbright; landscapes in oil and water colour.

TERRIS, JOHN (1865-1914).   Born, Glasgow; exhibited Birmingham, R.A. from 1890, landscapes and seascapes in oil and watercolour, especially Fife, Yorkshire and Norfolk. R.W.S.; R.S.W., R.I. Died, Glasgow. **£25-42, 10-34 (w).**

THOMAS, GROSVENOR (1855-1923). Born, Sydney (Australia); arrived in Glasgow 1885/6; self-taught, influenced by Corot, Daubigny and the Barbizons; mills were a favourite subject. R.S.W., 1892; S.S.A., 1893. **£140.**

THOMSON, ADAM BRUCE (1885-1976). Studied at Edinburgh School of Art; studied in Paris and Madrid, 1910; President, S.S.A., 1936 and R.S.W., 1954-1962. A.R.S.A., 1937; R.S.A., 1946; O.B.E., 1963; Hon. R.S.W., 1968. **£40, 50-60 (w).**

THOMSON, JOHN MURRAY (1885-1974). Born, Ayr; studied Edinburgh and Paris (Academie Julien); taught animal drawing Edinburgh College of Art; in demand for commissions for animal paintings. A.R.S.A., 1939; R.S.A., 1957. **£21-78, 50 (w).**

THOMSON, Rev. JOHN, known as "Thomson of Duddingston" (1778-1840). Born, Dailly, Ayrshire, where he succeeded his father as minister; in 1805 removed to parish of Duddingston, nr. Edinburgh; pupil of Alex. Nasmyth (*q.v.*); painted romantic landscapes and coast scenes. H.R.S.A., 1826. **£42-500.**

THOMSON, LESLIE (1851-1929). Born, Aberdeen; painter of landscapes and seascapes. R.W.S.; H.R.O.I.

THOMSON, WILLIAM JOHN (1771-1845). Lived and worked in Edinburgh; exhibited R.S.A. from 1830; landscapes, mural studies, portraits, historical scenes, etc. R.S.A., 1829. **£150.**

THORBURN, ROBERT (1815-1885). Born, Dumfries; moved to England; painted miniatures and, in later life, oil portraits; with Sir W. Ross, one of the last of old school of miniature painters. Died, Tonbridge.

TORRANCE, JAMES (1859-1916). Born, Glasgow; worked in London as book illustrator; settled in Glasgow and painted portraits. Died, Helensburgh.

TRAQUAIR, Mrs PHOEBE ANN (1852-1936). Born, Dublin; daughter of Dr Moss; studied at Dublin School of Art; in 1872 married Dr Ramsay Traquair, who became Keeper of Nat. Hist., R.S. Museum, Edinburgh; after many years of family life, took up embroidery, illuminations and enamel work; well known for her mural paintings. H.R.S.A., 1920. Died, Edinburgh.

VALLANCE, WILLIAM FLEMING (1827-1904). Born, Paisley; studied Trustees' Art School under Robert Scott Lauder (*q.v.*); painter of the sea and shipping. A.R.S.A., 1875; R.S.A., 1881. **£40 (w).**

WAIT, RICHARD (died 1732). Born, Scotland; pupil of the younger Scougall and said to have worked under Kneller; painted numerous Highland portraits and still life.

WALES, JAMES (1748-1795). Born, Peterhead; portraits.

WALKER, DAME ETHEL (1861-1951). Born, Edinburgh; lived and worked at Robin Hood Bay,

Yorkshire, and in London; particularly noted for portraits and still life. A.R.A., R.B.A., R.P. Died, London. **£70.**

WALLS, WILLIAM (1860-1942). Born, Dunfermline; trained at the School of Design, R.S.A. Life Classes and Antwerp under Verlat; regular exhibitor and contributor to *The Evergreen*; passionately interested in animals and produced some fine animal paintings; also some figure paintings, portraits and landscapes in the Highlands. A.R.S.A., 1901; R.S.A., 1914; R.S.W. Died, Edinburgh. **£10-310.**

WALTON, CECILE (1891-1956). Born, Glasgow; daughter of E. A. Walton (*q.v.*) and married Eric Robertson (*q.v.*); marriage broke down 1923. Died, Edinburgh.

WALTON, EDWARD ARTHUR (1860-1922). Born, Renfrewshire; student at Glasgow School of Art and Düsseldorf; worked with members of Glasgow School, MacGregor, Guthrie and Crawhall; painted portraits and landscape, in oil and watercolour; moved to London, 1894; settled in Edinburgh, 1904. A.R.S.A., 1889; R.S.A., 1905; R.S.W., 1885; P.R.S.W., 1915. Died, Edinburgh. **£340-1,450, 120 (w).**

WATSON, GEORGE (1767-1837). Born, Overmains, Berwickshire; worked under Alex. Nasmyth (*q.v.*) and for two years in London under Reynolds; settled in Edinburgh and practised as portrait painter; first President of the Scottish Academy, 1826, and held office till his death. Died, Edinburgh.

WATSON, WILLIAM SMELLIE (1796-1874). Foundation Academician; lived and worked in Edinburgh; exhibited R.S.A. from 1827; specialised exclusively in portraiture. R.S.A., 1826.

WATT, GEORGE FIDDES (1873-1960). Born, Aberdeen; studied Gray's School of Art and R.S.A. Schools; exhibited R.S.A. and R.A., 1906-1930; lived in London and, later, Aberdeen. A.R.S.A., 1910; R.S.A., 1924; R.P. Died, Aberdeen.

WELLS, WILLIAM PAGE ATKINSON (1872-1923). Born, Glasgow; "sensitively observed and skilfully painted landscapes marked by much quiet sentiment and fine feeling" (Caw: *Scottish Painting*). Died, Isle of Man. **£100-300.**

WEST, DAVID (1868-1936). Born and worked in Lossiemouth.

WHYTE, D. MACGREGOR (1866-1953). Born, Oban; studied in Glasgow, Paris and Antwerp; exhibited R.S.A., G.I.; seascapes and portraits in oil. **£18-22.**

WILKIE, Sir DAVID (1785-1841). Born, Cults, Fife; studied at Trustees' Academy, Edinburgh; at age 19 exhibited "Pitlessie Fair", containing 140 figures, besides painting portraits; moved to London, 1805, and entered R.A. Schools; visited Paris 1814, Holland 1816 and made prolonged visit to Continent, 1825-1828; painted portraits, genre subjects and historical compositions; with Geddes was responsible for revival of etching. A.R.A.,

1809; R.A., 1811 (at age 26); King's Limner for Scotland, 1823; Painter-in-Ordinary to King George IV, 1830; knighted, 1836. In 1840 set out for Holy Land and Egypt; died on return voyage, off Gibraltar; buried at sea. (See Turner's "Peace-Burial at Sea" in Tate Gallery.)

WILLIAMS, HUGH WILLIAM (1773-1829). known as "Grecian Williams". Born at sea; settled in Edinburgh and practised as watercolour painter; for several years travelled in Greece and Italy; published *Travels in Italy, Greece, etc.,* 1820, and *Views in Greece,* 1827-1829. Died, Edinburgh. **£80 (w), 220 (w—1975).**

WILLIAMS, JOHN FRANCIS (1785-1846). Born, Perthshire; foundation member Scottish Academy; scene painter in London and Edinburgh. R.S.A., 1826. Died, Glasgow.

WILLISON, GEORGE (1741-1797). Born, Edinburgh; sent by an uncle to study in Rome; on return settled in London, and from 1767 exhibited at R.A.; painted portraits; in India, 1774-80; Edinburgh, 1785-1797.

WILSON, ANDREW (1780-1848). Born, Edinburgh; after instruction from Nasmyth, studied at R.A. Schools, London, and in Italy; at Genoa, on second visit, 1803-1806; on return, became professor of drawing at Sandhurst, and in 1818 appointed master of Trustees' Academy, Edinburgh; returned Italy 1826, for rest of his life; painted landscapes. Died on a visit to Edinburgh.

WILSON, DAVID FORRESTER (1873-1950). Born, Glasgow; exhibited R.S.A., Glasgow Institute, Liverpool and U.S.A.; portraits and decorative subjects; large decorative panel in Glasgow Corpn. Banqueting Hall; A.R.S.A., 1922; R.S.A., 1932. Died, Glasgow.

WILSON, GEORGE (1848-1890). Born, Cullen; studied Heatherley, R.A. and Slade Schools; worked in London and travelled on the Continent; landscapes and allegorical pictures.

WILSON, GEORGE WASHINGTON (1823-1893). Born, Waulkmill of Carnoustie (Banffshire); executed some painting but more notable as a pioneer photographer.

WILSON, P. MACGREGOR (died 1928). Born, Glasgow; exhibited London galleries from 1890; President of Glasgow Art Club; travelled extensively and painted wide range of subjects; R.S.W. **£11-45.**

WILSON, ROBERT (born 1889). Also known as "Scottie" Wilson; born, Glasgow; lived in Scotland, Toronto and London; designed stained glass and painted imaginative subjects; work shown internationally; signs work "Scottie".

WINGATE, Sir JAMES LAWTON (1846-1924). Born, Kelvinhaugh; self-taught but entered Edinburgh School of Art, 1872 and R.S.A. Life School, 1874; painted landscapes and scenes with incidents of pastoral life; noted for his sunset effects. A.R.S.A., 1879; R.S.A., 1889; P.R.S.A., 1919, and knighted. **£35-300.**

WINTOUR, JOHN CRAWFORD (1825-1882). Born, Edinburgh; studied at Trustees' Academy; painted portraits, but about 1850 turned his attention to landscape work. A.R.S.A., 1859. **£24-270, 10-20 (w).**

WISHART, PETER (1846-1932). Born, Aberdour; studied Royal Institution, Edinburgh, and Antwerp under Verlat, together with such artists as MacGeorge, Mackie, Hornel and Walls (*q.v.*); landscapes and Highland scenes. A.R.S.A., 1925.

WOOLNOTH, ALFRED (*fl.* 1870-1890). Exhibited R.S.A.; lived Edinburgh and Hampstead; painted extensively in Scotland.

WOOLNOTH, CHARLES N. (1815-1906). Born, London; English School painter but worked in Scotland; landscapes. R.S.W. **£85-125 (w).**

WRIGHT, JOHN MICHAEL (1625-1700). Born, Scotland; said to have been pupil of Jamesone and to have gone to England about age 17; afterwards in Italy; returned to England; described by Evelyn as "the famous painter, Mr Wright"; one of Court Painters after Restoration; painted portraits.

WRIGHT, MARGARET (1884-1957). Born, Ayr; studied G.S.A.; exhibited Glasgow Institute, R.S.A. and Paisley Institute; mainly landscapes. Died, Gourock.

WYLIE, Miss KATE (1877-1941). Born, Skelmorlie; studied G.S.A.; exhibited R.A., R.S.A., G.I.; portraits, flowers and landscapes. **£26-40.**

WYSE, HENRY TAYLOR (1870-1951). Born, Glasgow; studied Dundee School of Art, G.S.A. and Paris; exhibited R.S.A., G.I.; London and provinces; lectured and wrote on art; lived Edinburgh; painted landscapes in all media.

YOUNG, Miss BESSIE INNES (*fl.* 1890-1930). Born, Glasgow; studied G.S.A. and Paris (Academie Delecluse); exhibited R.S.A., G.I.; landscapes, genre and still life; S.S.W.A.

YOUNG, R. CLOUSTON (*fl.* 1920s). Lived and worked in Glasgow and, later, Ardrossan; exhibited R.S.W., G.I.; watercolours; R.S.W. **£80.**

YOUNG, WILLIAM (1845-1916). Lived and worked in Glasgow; exhibited London and Scotland; landscapes, usually in watercolour; R.S.W. **£160.**

YOUNGER, JANE (1863-1955). Born, Glasgow; studied G.S.A., 1890-1900; shared studio with Bessie Young (*q.v.*) and Annie French (*q.v.*). Died, Crawford, Lanarkshire.

YULE, WILLIAM JAMES (1869-1900). Born, Dundee; son of a whaling captain; studied at Westminster School of Art, at Paris, and in Spain; worked for a few years in Edinburgh and in London, 1897-1898, but with precarious health.

SUGGESTED FURTHER READING

The following books are recommended to the reader who would like to discover more about the artists listed. The first part of the Bibliography consists of books which are in print and which should be readily available; the second part is made up of books which are now out of print. Although they are sometimes to be found in antiquarian bookshops and at auction, prices are usually high and it may only be possible to consult them at a library.

IN PRINT

SIR JAMES L. CAW: *Scottish Painting Past and Present* (1908); a facsimile reprint by Kingsmead Reprints, Bath, is now available.

DAVID AND FRANCINA IRWIN: *Scottish Painters at Home and Abroad, 1700-1900;* a recent appraisal published 1965 by Faber & Faber, London.

FRANK RINDER: *The Royal Scottish Academy 1826-1916* (1917); a facsimile reprint by Kingsmead Reprints of Rinder's list of Academicians and Associates and the work they exhibited during this period.

DAVID MARTIN: *The Glasgow School of Painting* (1897); reprinted 1976 by Paul Harris Publishing. Uniform with this book.

DR T. J. HONEYMAN: *Three Scottish Colourists* (1950); reprinted 1977 by Paul Harris Publishing. Deals with Cadell, Hunter and Peploe. Uniform with this book.

AGNES MACKAY: *Arthur Melville 1855-1904;* published by F. Lewis, Leigh-on-Sea, 1951.

ADRIAN BURY: *Joseph Crawhall, The Man and the Artist* (1959); published by Charles Skilton Ltd., London. A handsomely produced volume.

GEORGE BRUCE: *Anne Redpath* (1974); Edinburgh University Press, the first in the Modern Scottish Painters series.

T. ELDER DICKSON: *W. G. Gillies* (1974); Edinburgh University Press, second in the Modern Scottish Painters series.

The reader should also be referred to the Scottish Arts Council, 19 Charlotte Square, Edinburgh, who have a number of exhibition catalogues which may be of interest. Similarly, The Fine Art Society Ltd., 12 Great King Street, Edinburgh, have produced some very elegant and informative catalogues to accompany their exhibitions of work by Scottish painters. Periodically, Glasgow Art Gallery and Museums Association publish *The Scottish Art Review,* which is well worthy of study (available from The Art Gallery, Kelvingrove, Glasgow).

OUT OF PRINT

PROFESSOR BALDWIN BROWN: *The Glasgow School of Painters* (1908).

ROBERT BRYDALL: *Art in Scotland — Its Origins and Progress* (1889).

SIR JAMES L. CAW: *Sir James Guthrie — A Biography* (1932).

SIR JAMES L. CAW: *William McTaggart* (1917).

STANLEY CURSITER: *Peploe — An Intimate Memoir of an Artist and his Work* (1947).

J. D. FERGUSSON: *Modern Scottish Painting* (1943).

IAN FINLAY: *Art in Scotland* (1948).

SIDNEY GILPIN: *Sam Bough, R.S.A., Some Account of his Life and Works* (1905).

C. GURLITT: *Malerei in Schottland* (1893).

HILDA ORCHARDSON GRAY: *Life of Sir William Quiller Orchardson* (1925).

W. E. HENLEY: *A Century of Artists* (1888).

DR T. J. HONEYMAN: *Introducing Leslie Hunter* (1937).

SIR JOHN LAVERY: *The Life of a Painter* (1940).

W. D. McKAY: *The Scottish School of Painting* (1906).

ROBERT MACLEOD: *Charles Rennie Mackintosh* (1968); published by Country Life Books and, incredibly, remaindered.

WALTER SHAW SPARROW: *John Lavery and his Work* (1912).

GLEESON WHITE: *Master Painters* (1898).

The End